The Next Step
A Practical Guide to College and Career
Success

A workbook for teens and adults who want to build a fulfilling life.

Kristi Smith, MBA

http://thenextstep.site

Copyright © 2017 by Kristi Smith

Updated version 3.0 2022

Cover by Raven Rucker

All rights reserved. No portion of this book may be

reproduced in any form without written

permission from the author.

ISBN: 1548431591
ISBN-13: 978-1548431594

This book is dedicated to my students. I am grateful to be a part of your life. I wish you great success in finding your personal fulfillment by taking the next step.

THE NEXT STEP

A PRACTICAL GUIDE TO COLLEGE AND CAREER SUCCESS

Introduction: About the Next Step   Pg. 1

Step 1: Set Goals   Pg. 6

Step 2: Define Success   Pg. 9

Step 3: Identify Your Values   Pg. 11

Step 4: Recognize Your Strengths   Pg. 13

Step 5: Consider the Money Factor   Pg. 21

Step 6: Evaluate Job Outlook   Pg. 39

Step 7: Explore Possible Careers   Pg. 42

Step 8: Research/Analyze Careers   Pg. 47

Step 9: Make an Education Plan   Pg. 71

Step 10: Get the Job   Pg. 108

The Last Step: Summary   Pg. 134

Thank you to my mom for always encouraging me to write, be myself, and go for the things I want in life. Thank you to my husband for supporting me and being a good listener. Thank you to Raven Rucker for her creativity and time in creating the cover. Thank you to Bethany Drosendahl for her encouragement and advice.

INTRODUCTION: ABOUT THE NEXT STEP

In this book, you will be able to:
- ✓ Step 1 Set Goals
- ✓ Step 2 Define Success
- ✓ Step 3 Identify Your Values
- ✓ Step 4 Recognize Your Strengths
- ✓ Step 5 Consider the Money Factor
- ✓ Step 6 Evaluate Job Outlook
- ✓ Step 7 Explore Possible Careers
- ✓ Step 8 Research and Analyze Careers
- ✓ Step 9 Make an Education Plan
- ✓ Step 10 Get the Job

Let's take the next step!
It is important to ask some essential questions:

What do I want? Cast a vision for the future and set goals

Who am I? Discover my personality, values, and strengths

How do I want to live? Consider my desired lifestyle/budget

How to get the job I want? Which path will I take to prepare and how will I showcase my skills and experience to get the job?

Taking the next step is about designing an ideal plan. Why not ask for what you want? You may get it! Learn about yourself and discover what success means to you. Find the facts and create a plan to follow. This plan will become the starting point for life's adventure. This adventure may take some twists and turns. Be willing to take the twists and turns as a chance for new opportunity. I believe that if you start off with a solid direction, this journey will have the best possible outcome.

Invest in yourself, build your life, impact those around you.

🚶 Step One: Set Goals
WHERE DO YOU WANT TO GO?

✏️ **Consider it:** Why is it important to set goals for the future?

_____

_____

_____

To take the next step, it is important to begin with the end in mind.

Activity: What are you doing in your life?

Who is your favorite teacher from the past? Mr./Mrs._____

If you don't have a favorite teacher, who is a relative or friend you haven't seen in a long time?_____

Scenario: *It has been 15 years since you graduated from high school. You are shopping at the grocery store. As you turn down the isle the shopping cart collides into another cart.*

🛒 *Oh I'm so sorry." Says the other shopper. You make eye contact and ask, "don't I know you?" "Yes!" It is so great to see you! It has been so long, what have you been doing in your life?"*

What do you say? Create a conversation on the next page.

Use the following sentence stems to have a conversation:

"It is great to see you too Mr./Mrs. _____"

"I graduated from _____high school in 20_ _."

"After that I studied _____(major-area of interest) at _____."

"I am now working as a:_____"

"I like it because…"

"I have a wonderful single life (or) wonderful family" (describe)…

"I live in_____"(city, state, or different country)

"I like it there because…"

"I have done some great/fun things including…"

"I am proudest of…"

"It was so nice to see you!. Wow! I am so proud of all that you have accomplished." Said the teacher.

You can build any life you want! What do you want? Who do you want to be?

Let's find out together and take the next step!

What are some things you hope to accomplish?

Some people like to set goals by creating a bucket list. However, life (I hope) is too long to list everything you want to do be for you DIE! These goals become a "someday" list instead of a focus. Instead, focus on the goal right in front of you.

✏ Consider it: Create a _modified_ "bucket list," list *10 things to accomplish* **in the next 10 years**:

1.
2.
3.
4.
5.
6.
7.
8.
9.
10.

Goals are a big part of finding fulfillment in life. Consider what your life may look like and the things you hope to accomplish, and it will give you an idea of what is important to you. Think about what fulfillment and success means to you. If you can identify this, you will be more likely to find what makes you happy in life and your career.

Make "someday" a reality!
Take small steps to reach each goal

Large or small, each goal can be attainable by breaking it up into small pieces.

Rules of goal setting:

1) **Focus:** center your effort on a few goals at a time. Decide <u>what</u> is important at the time to focus on.

> "A goal properly set is halfway reached."
> —Abraham Lincoln

2) **Put it in writing:** "Goals that are not written down are just wishes." –Unknown. Write your goals down and put them somewhere you will see them as a reminder.

3) **Make a plan:** find out what it takes to make it happen and do it! Most goals that are left unaccomplished are due to fear of the unknown. Conquer the unknowns through research and planning!

4) **Use SMART goals:** SMART is a well-known format to ensure a well-planned goal. It is used in academics, by individuals and businesses.

Apply it: Focus on three goals by writing them down:

Personal goal: _____

Educational goal: _____

Career goal: _____

How to write SMART goals:

S	**SPECIFIC**-Be <u>exact</u> in what you intend to do. **Begin with "I will"** instead of "I would like to." Be firm that you intend to do it.
M	**MEASURABLE**-Create a checklist of things that will help you get to your end goal
A	**ATTAINABLE**-Describe why exactly the goal is possible; it could be because of your "to do" list or deadline.
R	**RELEVANT**-Is it important to you right now and for long term plans? **OR** **RESEARCH**-Get the facts that will help you reach your goal. This will help get rid of the "unknowns" that generate fear.
T	**TIME-BOUND**- Give it a deadline to make it *actually* happen instead of "someday."

Analyze it: Which part of SMART do you think is the most important, why?

_____
_____
_____

Example:

S	"I will" go to Paris
	— (not I "want to" travel) It is SPECIFIC
M	To make this happen I will need to get a passport, save $2500, book my trip, learn some French.
A	It is attainable because I have a job and can save $200 per month until my booking deadline in 12.5 months.
R	I will research the facts of cost, how to get a passport, where I want to stay/activities, French classes.
T	I will go to Paris by July 15th

Apply it: *Write a SMART goal for something important to your life now*

S	I will
M	To make this happen I will
A	It is attainable because
R	I will research the facts of
T	I will do this by

Apply it: *Write a SMART goal for something important to your future*

S	I will
M	To make this happen I will
A	It is attainable because
R	I will research the facts of
T	I will do this by

Review it: <u>Check your work.</u> Did you follow the rules?

- ✓ Did you focus on <u>one</u> goal?
- ✓ Is your goal specific enough to know when you have accomplished it?
- ✓ Do you have checklist of things to do to make your goal happen?
- ✓ Do you have a deadline to make it happen instead of "someday?"

Step Two: Define Success

[**40 hours** a week, from the age of 20-65 and gets two weeks of vacation every year. In that time, the average person will have worked a total of **90,360 hours** of their life.]

Fact: 90,360 hours is spent <u>working!</u>

Make up your mind to be fulfilled; not miserable!

Fact: According to data by Gallup, only <u>13 percent</u> of employees are "engaged" in their jobs, or emotionally invested in their work and focused on helping their organizations improve.

 Evaluate it: Why do you think so many people hate their jobs?

_____

_____

Ask yourself the right questions to find something you would find "engaging."

What does success mean to you?

> *"Don't aim for success, if you want it; just do what you love and believe in, and it will come naturally."* David Frost

Your values and passion can help to determine how you define success!

✏️ **ACTIVITY**: Formulate a mission statement to live by: This a declaration of what you believe in and hope to accomplish as an overall view based on what you value in life.

Example:

"My mission statement is to have a fulfilling and balanced personal and professional life. I need to have a close relationship with my family and savor the time spent together. It is important to me to nurture and inspire those around me to make a difference in their lives. I am not afraid to try something new and will never stop learning and growing."

Consider it: What do you think fuels you? What are your driving factors in life?

✏️ My Mission Statement is:

_____
_____
_____
_____
_____

Step Three: Identify career values that matter!

Career values are important factors that impact your daily life based on your career choice.

Check the ones that are the most important to you:
- ☐ **Accomplishment:** achieving something or making an impact
- ☐ **Advancement:** moving up in the ranks of your career
- ☐ **Benefits:** health insurance, retirement benefits, expense accounts etc. provided by the company
- ☐ **Challenge:** accomplishing something that isn't easy
- ☐ **Clothing:** what do you want to wear every day? Professional attire, casual, visible tattoos, flip flops? Clothing is a major clue for your desired environment.
- ☐ **Commitment/identity:** do you want to embody the title you have? Example: doctor
- ☐ **Communication:** is it important to you to be able to talk to people in your duties?
- ☐ **Creativity:** do you have the need to create something or ideas?
- ☐ **Education/training:** learning new things or continuing education for your career
- ☐ **Environment:** conservative/liberal
- ☐ **Family:** time with family, schedule flexibility, or family oriented environment
- ☐ **Flexibility:** scheduling, working from home or other places, deadline flexibility
- ☐ **Fun/adventure:** excitement in your duties or environment
- ☐ **Homework:** do you take your work home with you? Is this something you are unwilling to do?
- ☐ **Independence:** preference to work without immediate supervision or not interacting with people
- ☐ **Innovation:** being part of the next new thing or idea
- ☐ **Integrity/morals/ethics:** are you unwilling to go against your morals?
- ☐ **Justice/Fairness:** do you need to stand for justice in your community?
- ☐ **Leadership:** taking on a management role or lead in your duties
- ☐ **Location/Re-location:** are you unwilling to move to a new location? Is there a specific geographic location where you desire to live?
- ☐ **Making a difference:** helping someone/something or making an impact
- ☐ **Order:** having structure in your job
- ☐ **People:** being able to interact with people
- ☐ **Prestige/power:** holding a title or leadership role
- ☐ **Professionalism:** working in a professional environment

- ☐ **Requirements:** how much education are you willing to complete to get the job?
- ☐ **Safety:** unwillingness to sacrifice your personal safety or others
- ☐ **Schedule:** flexible schedule, shift preference, holidays/weekends etc.
- ☐ **Serenity:** peaceful environment
- ☐ **Stability/demand:** high need in the community for your position to keep you employed
- ☐ **Stress:** low/medium/high (busy) stress?
- ☐ **Travel:** do you like to be away from home or are you unwilling to travel?
- ☐ **Variety:** variation in job duties, environment, or people
- ☐ **Money**-Determine a salary range that is right for you in the "Money Factor" section.

✎ <u>Choose 5 career values</u> that are MOST important to you from the ones you checked:

1) _____
2) _____
3) _____
4) _____
5) _____

✎ **Consider it:** Everyone needs money to pay the bills, but is there another reason you want money?

Do you want money to provide for your family? To prove that you are successful? To be able to do fun things? To be able to have nice things?

What do YOU want money for? _____

Step Four: Recognize Your Strengths

What are your personal strengths? If you can recognize them, you will be able to utilize them. Start by being okay with the fact that YES, it is okay to be awesome! However, there is a difference between being confident and being cocky.

You are your own worst critic and we tend to focus on our weaknesses, when we SHOULD focus on our strengths. Focus on your strengths!

Believe in yourself!

Start by asking people who know you well what they think are your strengths. Other people see you in a different way than you see yourself.

ACTIVITY: Ask **at least 3 different people** (family, friend, authority figure) that you have known for at least 2 years what they think you're good at. (They can give you more than 1 answer).

List 5 strengths AND who said it: "what do you think I am good at?"

1) _____   Who said it: _____

2) _____   Who said it: _____

3) _____   Who said it: _____

4) _____   Who said it: _____

5) _____   Who said it: _____

List anything people ask your help with because you are good at it:_____
_____
_____

ACTIVITY: Circle any of the following that come to you easily:

Summarize it: List your top 5 strengths from the list, what people told you, or what they ask your help with. What are your greatest personal strengths?

1)_____
2)_____
3)_____
4)_____
5)_____

- Adaptability
- Attentiveness
- Attention to detail
- Analyzing
- Art
- Athleticism
- Communication
- Conflict Resolution
- Creativity
- Critical Thinking
- Decision Making
- Delegation
- Empathy
- Fast Learning
- Future Thinking
- Imagination/ideas
- Initiative
- Innovation
- Inspiring
- Integrity / Honesty
- Jokes / Humor
- Language learning/speaking
- Leadership
- Listening
- Logic
- Math
- Motivating
- Music
- Negotiating
- Networking (face to face)
- Networking (online)
- Organization
- Persuasion
- Planning
- Problem Solving
- Project Management
- Public Speaking
- Reading
- Research
- Self-motivation
- Spatial intelligence
- Social Intelligence
- Story Telling
- Teaching / Training
- Technology
- Visualization
- Writing

Your Personality

Understanding your personality is a *key* to self-awareness as well as understanding and getting along with others.

 ACTIVITY: Circle the ones that sound most like you:

Communicator-like to talk or write

Problem solver-fixing things/issues

Planner- setting goals/managing time

Manager-delegating/planning tasks

Logical thinker-analyzing information

Entertainer-perform to evoke emotion

Listener-good at really hearing people

Creator-building things or creating projects from ideas

Nurturer- taking care of others

Creative thinker-generating ideas

Server-like to help or serve people

Advocate-seek justice and righteousness

Relationship builder-understanding of people's feelings and motivations

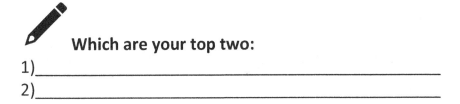 Which are your top two:
1)_____
2)_____

These could be great clues to your career fulfillment. Look for these to be fulfilled in your job duties.

Myers Briggs is an excellent tool in understanding four dimensions of your personality and differences with others.

✏️ **ACTIVTY:** *Google* "Free Myers Briggs personality test" for your personality test:

Myers Briggs personality 4-letter combination: _____(example: ENTJ)
Read about your strength traits.

List 5 strength traits you agree with:
1)_____
2)_____
3)_____
4)_____
5)_____

✏️ **ACTIVTY:** *Google* "Careers for _ _ _ _" for your 4-letter combination (e.g. ENTJ)

List 1-5 careers suggested that may be of interest to you
1)_____
2)_____
3)_____
4)_____
5)_____

✏️ **Evaluate it:** From your reading, what do you think are the most important factors in your career that will make you feel fulfilled?

_____

_____

Myers Briggs Types Summarized: [1]

Extrovert vs. Introvert

E (Extrovert)	I (Introvert)
<ul><li>Energized by being around people</li><li>Expose their feelings</li><li>Discuss a wide range of thought-many ideas at once</li><li>Thinks aloud</li><li>Likes to talk face to face</li></ul>	<ul><li>Energized by being alone or with few people</li><li>Concealed feelings, hard to read</li><li>Focuses on one idea in depth</li><li>Appreciates advance warning of discussion topics</li><li>Prefers written communication</li></ul>

Adapted from MBTI Basics

Evaluate it: Explain the difference in the way extroverts and introverts prefer to communicate?

_____

_____

_____

Apply it: Give an example of someone you know who is opposite of your E/I: How are they different?

_____

_____

_____

---

[1]"My MBTI Results," *The Myers & Briggs Foundation*, 2014, http://www.myersbriggs.org/my-mbti-personality-type/my-mbti-results/.

Sensor vs. Intuiter

S (Sensor)	N (Intuiter)
• Focuses on the present here and now • What is practical and the facts • Likes to get to the point • Prefers stability and routine • Step by step	• Focuses on the future and what could be • Uses gut feeling to guide decisions • Imaginative and abstract • Interested in doing new things • Focused on meaning

Evaluate it: Explain the differences of what the S/N pay attention to:

_____

_____

_____

Apply it: Give an example of someone you know who is opposite of your S/N: How are they different?

_____

_____

_____

Thinker vs. Feeler

T (Thinker)	F (Feeler)
• Uses their head (logic) in decisions • Objective (unbiased) • Firm, but fair	• Uses their heart (feeling) in decisions • Subjective (biased) based on experience • Merciful and compassionate

Define bias:

_____

_____

Evaluate it: Explain the differences of how the T/F make decisions:

_____

_____

_____

Apply it: Give an example of someone you know who is opposite of your T/F. How are they different?

_____

_____

_____

Judger Vs. Perceiver

J (Judger)	P (Perceiver)
• Plans their life • Organized and proactive • Likes to have control • Work before play	• Spontaneous • Open to change • Let life happen • Energized by approaching deadlines

Evaluate it: Explain the differences between the J/P in how they live their lives:

_____

_____

_____

_____

Apply it: Give an example of someone you know who is opposite of your J/P: How are they different?

_____

_____

_____

_____

Step Five: Consider The Money Factor

Choosing a career is all about fulfillment. There are many people who are fulfilled in their job without making a ton of money. However, it is a factor that affects life in a major way. Paying the bills is something we all must do. A person's lifestyle ideals need to be considered when choosing a career.

Usually we do not want to give up what we have become accustomed to. Take your parent's income into account and the lifestyle you are used to. Sometimes it can be shocking how fast money goes and which *needs* are actually *wants* and vice versa. We will consider the basics and ideals.

Basic Bills

What does it take to live on you own and simply survive? Here are *basic* monthly bills to consider:

ACTIVITY: How much do YOU think each costs per month for an adult?

Rent	$_____
Utilities	$_____
Food	$_____
Car payment	$_____
Gas	$_____
Car Insurance	$_____
Renters Insurance	$_____
Phone	$_____
Total	$_____

Consider the lifestyle YOU want to experience. What does it look like?

Rent

When choosing a place to live, first, consider your standards of living for: affordability, cleanliness, safety, and convenience. Which one are you willing to be most flexible?

Utilities (natural gas, water/waste water, electricity)

How big is the space (square feet)? How many bedrooms? How many people will be living there? Will any utilities be included in the rent?

Tip! Call the utility company when considering a place to buy or rent and ask how much the average bill is per month.

Groceries

Food is expensive! Make a list and shop wisely. Compare prices and value for what you get.

Tip! Look at the cost per unit on the shelf

Tip! Cut coupons and use store ads

Gas

When buying a car, consider the miles per gallon (MPG) it will consume!

Tip! Many gas stations have discount cards

CAR INSURANCE

This depends on the type of vehicle, your driving record, age etc. Shop around!!!

Tip! Shop around again every few years. Insurance companies complete for your business, and making a switch can be cheaper for you!

RENTERS INSURANCE

This insurance covers all of your personal belongings due to theft, fire etc.

Phone

What kind of service do you really need? Can you stay on a family plan? How long?

There is a difference between gross and net income. Understand your paycheck.

Gross income: Earnings before tax/deductions

Net income: Earnings after tax/deductions (*actual* $ you will receive)

Standard deductions: Federal Tax, State Tax, Medicare, Social Security

Possible deductions: Health insurance, dental, 401K

Example:

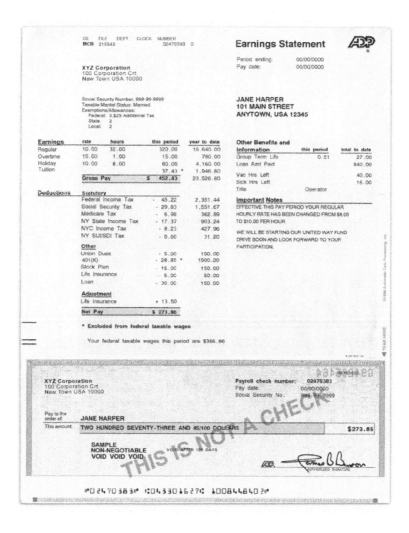

Tax Form W-4

What should I claim on my W4 when I start a new job 0 or Exempt?

This form can look intimidating if you don't know what to do.

Visit IRS.gov for more information:

Simply stated, the higher the number of allowances you claim, the less tax will be withheld from each paycheck.

Generally, *claiming 0* means more tax will be withheld resulting in a tax return.

Claiming *exempt* from having any Federal taxes withheld is possible if you earn less that the standard deduction for the year.

ACTIVITY: Calculate your paycheck. Find a job to pay bills to live on your own.

1. Find a specific <u>job you could get</u> **right now** to live on your own if you had to move out.

Google "how much does a _____ make at _____ (company) in _____ (your city)

Example: *How much does a team member make at Burger King in Denver Colorado?*

2. Your job title:_____ $_____ per hour

3. How many hours could you work per week?_____ (20-40 hours)

4. How much would you make per month? (4 weeks) $_____

Calculate YOUR paycheck
Hours per week_____ X $_____ =$_____ per week X 4 weeks in a month =$_____ monthly pay

Example: 40 hours per week X $20.00 per hour= $800 per week
　　　　　$800 per week x 4 weeks in a month=$2400
　　　　　=$2400 **Gross income (*before* tax)**

5. Multiply monthly income by 15% (estimated) for Federal Tax, Social Security, Medicare
   Total monthly income $_____ X .15 =$_____

Example: $2400 X .15 =$ 360

6. Total monthly income _____ -tax_____ = net income $_____

Example: $2400 - $240 = $2040 **NET income (*after* tax is withheld from your paycheck)**

Use your net income to create a budget

ACTIVITY: *To create a monthly budget, find a place to live on your own*

Where do I look?

1) Search online: www.apartments.com or www.ForRent.com

2) Ask family or friends for recommendations

3) Drive around your preferred neighborhood to find places available

FOR RENT

What should I consider?

1) Cost
   a. Landlords will usually require paystubs to prove consistent income where rent does not exceed 30% of your monthly net pay
   b. Do you need a roommate to cover the cost of rent? Will they be reliable?
2) Convenience
   a. Is the location close to places you need to go? Work? School? Stores? Family? Entertainment?
   b. Where will you do you laundry? Is there a washer/dryer? Laundry is expensive and a pain to haul dirty laundry to the laundry mat.
3) Safety
   a. What is the neighborhood like? Ask around before signing a lease?
4) Comfort
   a. Take a tour to make sure it meets your standards and your comfort level. You never know if you don't visit! I almost signed a lease once until I realized there were train tracks directly behind the house.

How do I get a lease?

1) Complete an application with the rental company or landlord
   a. Bring cash or check for the application fee
   b. Provide paystubs
   c. Be ready for a credit check. If you haven't built any credit a co-signer may be required (usually a parent).
   d. Bring reference letters from previous landlords or employers and be ready for a background check
2) Review the lease
   a. Be aware of how long the lease term is for. The contract may be 6 months or 1 year. You will have the opportunity to move when the lease is up. They may not raise your rent or make any changes to the contract during the lease.
3) Review the property
   a. Take note of any damages and take pictures to protect yourself from being charged for pre-existing damage.
4) Pay deposits
   a. This could be the equivalent of 3 month's rent.
   b. Be prepared to pay cash or check for first and last month's rent as well as a security deposit. A security deposit protects the landlord from damage you do to the property.
   c. Take good care of the property to get your security deposit refunded when you move out.
      d. If you have pets, a non-refundable deposit may be required.
   Example:

STANDARD LEASE AGREEMENT

This Agreement is between _____ [Landlord's Name] of _____ [Street Address] in the City of _____, State of _____, hereinafter known as the "Landlord"

AND

_____
_____

hereinafter known as the "Tenant(s)" agree to the following:

OCCUPANT(S). The Premises is to be occupied strictly as a residential dwelling with the following individual(s) in addition to the Tenant(s):

_____
_____

hereinafter known as the "Occupant(s)".

OFFER TO RENT. The Landlord hereby rents to the Tenant(s), subject to the following terms and conditions of this Agreement, a _____ [Type of residence such as Apartment, Home, Condo, etc.] with the following mailing address _____ [Street Address] in the City of _____, State of _____, consisting of ____ Bathroom(s) and ____ Bedroom(s) hereinafter known as the "Premises".

PURPOSE. The Tenant(s) and any Occupant(s) may only use the Premises as a residential dwelling. It may not be used for storage, the manufacturing of any type of food or product, a professional service(s), or for any commercial use unless otherwise stated in this Agreement.

ACTIVITY: *Find a place to live on your own*

Where you want to live? _____ House _____ Apartment _____ other

City: _____ State: _____

# of Bedrooms _____ **# of Bathrooms** _____

Amenities Included:

Gym? Pool? Utilities? Cable? Wi-fi? Garbage? Washer/Dryer? Other? _____

Do you have pets? Y/N Will they allow pets? Y/N Are there any pet fees or deposits? $_____

Rent per month $_____ **How many roommates?** _____

Your part of the rent $_____

ACTIVITY: Calculate your maximum expenses

Budgeting Guidelines: Use this to keep your budget manageable

Your net income from activity $_____

Net income x 30% = $_____ max rent

Net income x 10% = $_____ savings for emergencies

Utilities = rent x 15% = $_____ utilities (*estimation*)

  *call the utility company for actual est.

Net income x 15% = $_____ max car payment (avoid financing a car, use CASH)

ACTIVITY: **Create a budget for living on your own if you had to move out tomorrow.** Use my estimates, averages based on research or talk to family/friends:

Savings (10% of net income)	$_____	Save for emergencies!!!
Rent	$_____	Do NOT exceed 30% of net income
Utilities	$_____	May be included in apartment
Garbage	$_____	May be included in apartment ($25 est.)
Food	$_____	Shop smart! ($300-400 est.)
Car payment	$____0____	Avoid!!!!! Buy a car with cash
Gas	$_____	Buy a car that's good on gas! ($200 est.)
Renter's Insurance	$_____	Same company as car insurance ($25 est.)
Car Insurance	$_____	Shop around ($100-$300)
Phone	$_____	Shop around ($30-$100 est.)
Internet	$_____	Optional/may be incl. in apt. ($100 est.)
Cable/Satellite	$_____	Optional/may be incl. in apt. ($100)
Pets	$_____	Optional (food, vet bills etc. $50-$100 est.)
Gym	$_____	Optional/may be incl. in apt. 50 est.)
Total Expenses:	$_____	Add up!

Net Income per month after tax: $_____ - Total Expenses $_____ =$_____

You should have a money left over!

If not, find a better job, work more hours, get more roommates or do not move out.

How do I get a better job?

Get an education to gain knowledge and skills, work to gain more experience, network.

Finance
It is important to understand some concepts about credit when building your future. You may need to get a loan for a house or a car.

BUILDING CREDIT

Credit is built by borrowing money and paying it back on-time for at least 6 months.

CREDIT SCORE

Your credit score is *mostly* based on on-time, long-term payment history and how much of your available credit you use. It is recommended not to use more than 30% of your available credit. Pay off your bill in full each month to manage your allotment of available credit and avoid paying interest.

LOAN TERM

The period of time a loan is to be re-paid usually with regular scheduled payments. The longer the loan term, the more interest you will pay the lender over time.

INTEREST RATE

The current interest rate is determined by the federal government as a basis, then figured by the lender based on your credit score.

FINANCING A CAR

Figure out how much you can <u>really</u> afford before shopping. Either save up a lump sum to buy without financing or save for a big down payment. Don't let the dealership talk you into taking on more than you can handle. Go to your bank and get pre-approved for a car loan without the pressure of sales people. Keep your monthly payment less than 15% of your monthly net income.

GETTING A HOME LOAN

Go to your bank for pre-approval of a loan before shopping. The bank will want at least 2 years of steady work history and a good debt-to-income ratio. Keep your income higher than your debt. Do not exceed 30% of your monthly net income for your mortgage payments.

MONTHLY PAYMENT

Use an online payment calculator to figure out how much you would pay monthly for any loan using the current interest rate.

Take the *next* step! Envision your *future* lifestyle with a *career!*

 ACTIVITY: Calculate your career income

How much do you think you will earn per year in a career? $_____

> Google "How much does _____ (your career) earn on average per year" or "careers that make $_____ per year."

Annual income: $_____ divide by 12 to find monthly income: $_____/month

Put 6% away for retirement in your company 401k plan or other plan:
$_____ per month X .06%=$_____ (goes to retirement)

Subtract retirement from monthly income: $_____ monthly income-the 67% for retirement $_____ =$_____ monthly income after retirement

Now subtract an estimate for **health insurance** $300 for you or $700 for a family

Monthly income after retirement $_____ - _____ health insurance=$_____ =$_____

Now take out taxes:
Estimated taxes: 6.2% for Social Security/Medicare, 25% est. for progressive federal tax, and 6% est. state tax **=37% est.**

Monthly Income after retirement and health insurance $_____ X .37 est. tax and retirement (taxes will vary based on actual income) =$_____ taxes
Monthly Income after retirement and health insurance $_____ - $_____ taxes=$_____ **Net income**

Consider it: What kind of future lifestyle do you want?

2) Where do you want to live?_____(city)_____(state/country)
3) Will you be married? Y/N
4) Will you have children? Y/N   How many? _____
5) Do you have a career in mind? _____
6) How much do you think you will earn per year? $_____

ACTIVITY: Shop for your ideal future house on www.realtor.com

Where you want to live? _____House _____ Townhouse _____other_____

City:_____ State:_____

# of Bedrooms_____   **# of Bathrooms_____**

Total cost to buy: $_____

> Google "free mortgage calculator" Find your monthly mortgage payment based on current interest rates, and either a 15 or 30-year loan

Calculate Mortgage Payment

Example: $350,000   (Total cost)   4.0%   Interest rate %   30 years

$_____ (Total Cost)   ___% interest rate   _____years

Estimated monthly mortgage payment: $_____

Use this monthly mortgage amount on your future budget

✏️ **ACTIVITY:** Shop for your ideal **future** vehicle using www.kbb.com, www.edmunds.com , or www.NADA.com

Describe your vehicle: (Consider it...do you have kids?)

Year:_____ Make:_____ Model:_____

Example: Year: 2020   Make: Toyota   Model: Rav-4

Price of Vehicle: $_____

✏️ **ACTIVITY:** Calculate your monthly car payment

Remember, this should not exceed 15% of your <u>future</u> net income

> **Google "free auto loan calculator"** Find your monthly payment based on current interest rates for a traditional 60-month loan.

Tip: <u>always</u> get a shorter loan term if you can afford the payment! It can save you $$$ in interest!

Example: $25,000 (Price of Vehicle)   5 % Interest rate   60 months

Estimated monthly payment: $472

$_____ (Price of Vehicle)   ____% Interest rate   ____ months

Estimated monthly payment: $_____ Use this amount on you budget.

✏️ **ACTIVITY**: Create a **future** budget for your lifestyle with a **career**

Use my estimates, averages based on research, or talk to family/friends:

*You may **share** some of these expenses with your spouse or roommates!

Savings (10% of net income)	$_____	Save for emergencies!!!
*Mortgage **(from activity)**	$_____	Do NOT exceed 30% of net income
*Home Owners Insurance	$_____	(included in mortgage)
*Utilities	$_____	(Estimate 15% of mortgage)
*Garbage	$_____	($20 est.)
*Groceries	$_____	($300 per person est.)
Car payment **(from activity)**	$_____	Do NOT exceed 15% of net income
Gas	$_____	($200 est.)
Car Insurance	$_____	Shop around ($100 est.)
Phone	$_____	Shop around ($80 per person est.)
*Internet	$_____	Optional ($100 est.)
*Cable/Satellite	$_____	Optional ($100 est.)
*Pets	$_____	Optional ($50-$100 est.)
*Gym	$_____	Optional ($100-$200 family)
*Daycare	$_____	($400 per week/per child under 5)
Student loan	$_____	(calculate or estimate) Get scholarships!

Student Loan Calculator: Estimate Your Payments – Forbes Advisor

Total Expenses: $_____

Net income $_____ - $_____ total expenses =$_____

✏️ **Analyze it:** How do you feel about your future budget?

_____

Retirement

 Consider it: Why should I care about retirement now?

_____

_____

There are many different ways to plan for retirement. The most important thing is that you DO actually plan for it early. The hard fact is that you will grow older. As you age, it is likely that you will *not want to* or *not be able* to work full-time to earn money.

Terms to be aware of to plan for retirement:

RETURN ON INVESTMENT (ROI)

Your profit (return) on your money invested usually expressed as a percentage.

SIMPLE INTEREST

Profit earned from the principal (money you invested) multiplied by the interest rate.

    Principal x Interest Rate=Profit   Example: $1000 x 7% = $70

COMPOUND INTEREST

Profit earned from the principal (money you invested) PLUS the interest earned multiplied by the interest rate.

    Principal + profit earned x interest Rate=Profit   Example: $1000 + 70= 1070 x 7% = $74.90

Interest is earned over time. Find the best interest rate that compounds often and regularly.

    Which type of interest will give you the best ROI? _____

ACTIVITY: Find out how much money you will need to retire.

This is based on your typical lifestyle you are accustomed to. The ultimate goal would be to pay off your house and car before you reach retirement age to reduce the amount needed to pay your bills.

To find how much you'll need to retire multiply your desired annual income and the number of years you plan on being retired.

1. What is your typical annual salary based on career research? $_____

2. Calculate how many years you will need to draw from retirement to live:

    ➢ At what age do you want to retire? _____ (Age 67 is considered retirement age to receive full benefits.)

    ➢ What age do you think you will live to? _____(plan to at least 100!!!)

    Example: 100-67=33 years _____-_____=_____years

    ➢ How many years will you live on retirement?_____

    ➢ Calculate how much money you think you will need to earn by retirement age _____(annual salary) x_____(years retired) =$_____

    Example: $50,000 x 33= $ 1.6 million

ACTIVTY: *Google* "Investment Calculator" to answer these questions:
1) How long will it take to earn at least $1.6 million for retirement?_____

2) How much should you contribute for retirement each month? _____

3) By what age should you start saving for retirement by starting your career?_____

How do I invest to save for retirement?

Traditionally there are two options for your monthly contributions: 401 (k) or IRA

401 (k)

Where do I get one?

A 401K is a retirement plan usually provided through your employer. Your monthly retirement contributions are deducted from your paycheck and invested using a company selected investment firm.

> Bottom line...you don't really have to worry about it. Just say you want to do it!

Although this is becoming rare, some companies will match your contribution as a benefit. If you contribute 6% of your salary, the company will invest that amount.

Example: 6% of $3000 monthly salary=$180   You invest $180, they invest $180=$360

% of your salary that you should contribute:_____%

It is recommended to invest 6-15 % of your salary. At least contribute the maximum that your company will match for free!!!

Benefits of a 401 (k)

1) <u>Free money</u> from your employer (if they have a company match)

2) Lower your taxable income and you won't be taxed on the $ you contribute out of your paycheck

3) Grows tax-deferred (You do not pay taxes on the money earned over time

> However, be aware that you will pay tax on the money as you draw it out during retirement.

Individual Retirement Account (IRA)

If you don't have a 401 (k) at your company or just want to have multiple plans, open an IRA

Where do I get one?

Any investment firm and most banks offer IRAs. You can transfer (roll over) funds from a 401 (k) or start one with minimal investment. Read reviews online to find the best one for you.

You can have funds automatically sent from your bank account each month to contribute

There are two types of IRAs:

Traditional IRA

- This is just like a 401 (k) and has the same benefits except nobody is contributing $ but you. It is not provided by your employer.

Roth IRA

- There is no tax benefit on your paycheck when contributing, however, you will not pay tax when funds are drawn during retirement after interest has accrued.

Think about it like this...you pay tax on $200 each month instead of 1 million when you have earned interest on your investment.

There are numerous ways to plan for retirement. Just choose at least one and start early!

Step Six: Evaluate Job Outlook
Job outlook or job demand is the availability of jobs in a specific career field

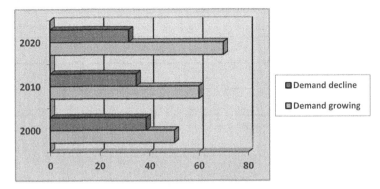

ACTIVITY: Watch the most current "Did You Know" video on YouTube. "Did you know" is a compilation of statistics about how the world is changing that may affect your future job outlook.

Evaluate it: What is going on in the world that will affect job outlook for your generation?

___
___
___
___
___

✏️ **Evaluate it:** use the charts below, why do you think these careers are declining?_____
_____
_____
_____

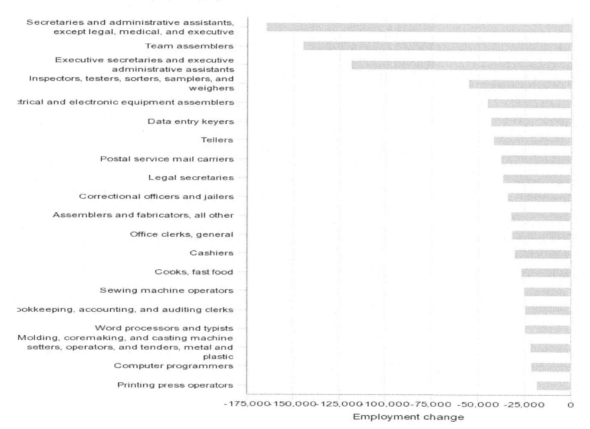

[2] "Projections of occupational employment, 2016–26," *Career Outlook,* U.S. Bureau of Labor Statistics, October 2017.

Evaluate it: use the charts below, why do you think these careers are growing?_____

_____

_____

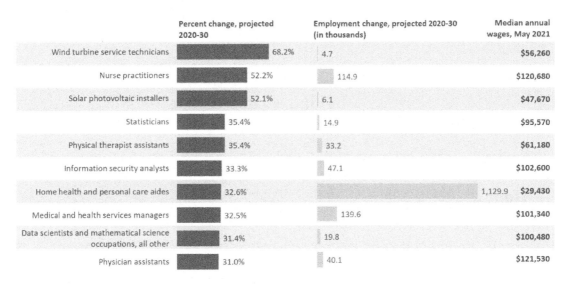

[3] "Projections of occupational employment, 2020-2030," *Career Outlook,* U.S. Bureau of Labor Statistics, July 2022.

Step Seven: Explore Possible Careers

ACTIVITY: Use www.mynextmove.org to explore possible careers

This resource is sponsored by the Department of Labor, developed by the National Center of O*NET Development. It is free and available to the public. [4]

Step One: Complete O*NET Interest Profiler (5-10 minutes)[5]

Go to "Tell us what you like to do." Click "Start" to answer questions about what interests you in a career. **Complete the O*NET Interest Profiler.**

In the purple section on the right...

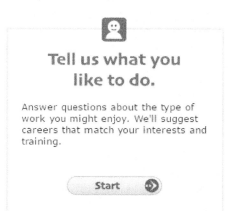

Circle your top 2-3 results: The interest profiler uses Holland Codes to determine career interest based on personality types (RIASEC).

Realistic   Investigative   Artistic   Social   Enterprising   Conventional

---

[4] "My Next Move." *National Center for O*NET Development*, http://www.mynextmove.org/.
[5] "O*NET Interest Profiler," *National Center for O*NET Development*, http://www.mynextmove.org/explore/ip.

Read the descriptions provided by O*NET:[6]

Realistic

People with **Realistic** interests like work that includes practical, hands-on problems and answers. Often people with **Realistic** interests do not like careers that involve paperwork or working closely with others.

They like:

- Working with plants and animals
- Real-world materials like wood, tools, and machinery
- Outside work

Investigative

People with **Investigative** interests like work that should do with ideas and thinking rather than physical activity or leading people.

They like:

- Searching for facts
- Figuring out problems

Artistic

People with **Artistic** interests like work that deals with the artistic side of things, such as acting, music, art, and design.

They like:

- Creativity in their work
- Work that can be done without following a set of rules

---

[6] "O*NET Interest Profiler," *National Center for O*NET Development*, http://www.mynextmove.org/explore/ip.

Social

People with **Social** interests like working with others to help them learn and grow. They like working with people more than working with objects, machines, or information.

They like:

- Teaching
- Giving advice
- Helping and being of service to people

Enterprising

People with **Enterprising** interests like work that should do with starting up and carrying out business projects. These people like taking action rather than thinking about things.

They like:

- Persuading and leading people
- Making decisions
- Taking risks for profits

Conventional

People with **Conventional** interests like work that follows set procedures and routines. They prefer working with information and paying attention to details rather than working with ideas.

They like:

- Working with clear rules
- Following a strong leader

Analyze it: How do these personality types describe your interests?

_____

_____

Step Two: Choose a "Job Zone"[7]

Click the "Next" button to move onto "Job Zones". Choose the "Job Zone" for the amount of preparation you are most comfortable completing for your future.

Read about each level to choose the best one for you!

Then Click "Next" (in the bottom right corner)

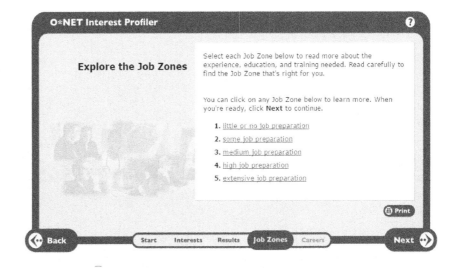

Click 'Next" to make your choice selecting the bubble.

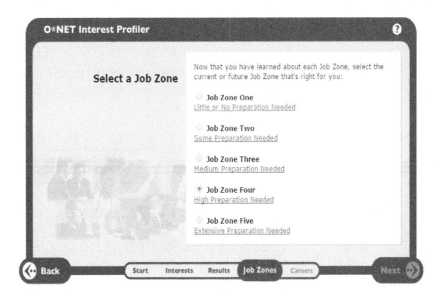

---

[7] "O*NET Interest Profiler," *National Center for O*NET Development*, http://www.mynextmove.org/explore/ip.

[8]Step Three: Explore careers by clicking on them.

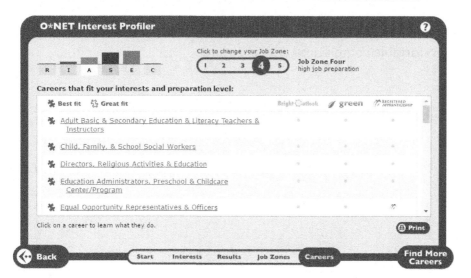

KEEP TRACK OF CAREERS OF INTEREST HERE!!!!

List Top 5-10 careers of interest:

1)_____ 6)_____

2)_____ 7)_____

3)_____ 8)_____

4)_____ 9)_____

5)_____ 10)_____

---

[8] O*NET Interest Profiler," *National Center for O*NET Development*, http://www.mynextmove.org/explore/ip.

Step Eight: Research and Analyze Careers

Choose 5 careers to research from your exploration:

1)_____
2)_____
3)_____
4)_____
5)_____

ACTIVITY: Research and analyze your top 5 careers

Complete the following research and analysis for each career using:

MY NEXT MOVE **www.mynextmove.org**.
My Next Move is sponsored by the U.S. Department of Labor. (Easiest way to find information)

BLS BUREAU OF LABOR STATISTICS, U.S. DEPARTMENT OF LABOR **www.bls.gov/ooh/** Bureau of Labor and Statistics Occupational Outlook Handbook (type your career in the search box)

careeronestop **www.careeronestop.org** is sponsored by the U.S. Department of Labor. It just uses a different format to find information. It is user friendly.

GLADEO **www.gladeo.org** is a fun website to explore careers by browsing by personality or watching videos.

Career #1 job title:_____

Are there some other titles this career may be called?
_____
_____

Daily Duties: What would you do on the job?
_____
_____
_____

Which of these duties would you enjoy the most? Are there any duties you wouldn't like?
_____
_____

Analyze it: Rate your satisfaction for how would spend your day:
    Meh 1 2 3 4 5 Amazing!

Knowledge: What would you need to study?
What would you have to study:
_____
_____

Analyze it: Rate your satisfaction:
    Meh 1 2 3 4 5 Amazing!

Skills and Abilities: What would you need to be good at?
_____
_____

Analyze it: Rate your satisfaction: Do your strengths match from pages 13-14?
    Meh 1 2 3 4 5 Amazing!

Education: How much preparation is necessary?
What are the requirements to get the job? Which level degree is necessary? example "Bachelor's Degree"

_____

What should you major in? "Google" "What should I major in to be a...?

Possible major(s): example "Accounting"

_____

_____

Analyze it: Rate your satisfaction:
Meh   1   2   3   4   5   Amazing!

Salary: What is the average salary per year?
$_____

Analyze it: Rate your satisfaction:
Meh   1   2   3   4   5   Amazing!

Job Outlook: How many jobs are projected for the future?

Click on **"See more details at O*NET Online"** at the bottom of the page for more detailed info to help answer this question.

Scroll to the bottom of the page to find "Wages & Employment Trends"

Wages & Employment Trends

Median wages (2015)	$32.45 hourly, $67,490 annual
State wages	Local Salary Info
Employment (2014)	2,751,000 employees
Projected growth (2014-2024)	Much faster than average (14% or higher)
Projected job openings (2014-2024)	1,088,400
State trends	Employment Trends
Top industries (2014)	Health Care and Social Assistance

Source: Bureau of Labor Statistics 2015 wage data and 2014-2024 employment projections. "Projected growth" represent (2014-2024). "Projected job openings" represent openings due to growth and replacement.

Click on "State trends"
What are the projections for your state? Select the state you wish to live in.

Employment (current)_____employees

Projected growth: _____% _____than average

Projected job openings: _____

State and National Trends				
United States	Employment		Percent Change	Projected Annual Job Openings [1]
	2014	2024		
Registered Nurses	2,751,000	3,190,300	+16%	108,840
Colorado	Employment		Percent Change	Projected Annual Job Openings [1]
	2014	2024		
Registered Nurses	44,840	59,660	+33%	2,350

[1] Projected Annual Job Openings refers to the average annual job openings due to growth and net replacement.
Occupation Trends FAQs

National Trends:

Employment (current)_____employees

Projected growth: _____% _____than average

Projected job openings: _____

Analyze it: Rate your satisfaction:

Meh 1 2 3 4 5 Amazing!

Personality: Does this sound like you?

Which personality traits does your career fulfill from pages 16-18 or RIASEC on page 42 from my next move?

_____

_____

Analyze it: Rate your satisfaction:

Meh 1 2 3 4 5 Amazing!

Career Values: Which career values do you think will be satisfied?

What are your top 5 career values you listed in **Step 3 from page 11**?

1) _____   Satisfied or Sacrificed?

2) _____   Satisfied or Sacrificed?

3) _____   Satisfied or Sacrificed?

4) _____   Satisfied or Sacrificed?

5) _____   Satisfied or Sacrificed?

Analyze it: Rate your satisfaction:

Meh 1 2 3 4 5 Amazing!

Evaluate it: What is your final analysis of this career. Discuss the pros and cons:

_____

_____

_____

Score Career #1

Tally the satisfaction rating for each section: (what number did you give each from Meh to Amazing?)

Duties: ___
Knowledge: ___
Skills & Abilities: ___
Education: ___
Major: ___
Salary: ___
Outlook: ___
Personality: ___
Career Values: ___
Total: ___

Career #2 job title: _____

Are there some other titles this career may be called?

_____
_____

Daily Duties: What would you do on the job?

_____
_____
_____

Which of these duties would you enjoy the most? Are there any duties you wouldn't like?

_____

Analyze it: Rate your satisfaction for how would spend your day:

Meh 1 2 3 4 5 Amazing!

Knowledge: What would you need to study?

What would you have to study:

_____
_____

Analyze it: Rate your satisfaction:

Meh 1 2 3 4 5 Amazing!

Skills and Abilities: What would you need to be good at?

_____

_____

Analyze it: Rate your satisfaction: Do your strengths match from pages 13-14?

Meh   1   2   3   4   5   Amazing!

Education: How much preparation is necessary?

What are the requirements to get the job? Which level degree is necessary? example "Bachelor's Degree"

_____

What should you major in? "Google" "What should I major in to be a…?

Possible major(s): example "Accounting"

_____

_____

Analyze it: Rate your satisfaction:

Meh   1   2   3   4   5   Amazing!

Salary: What is the average salary per year?

$_____

Analyze it: Rate your satisfaction:

Meh   1   2   3   4   5   Amazing!

Job Outlook: How many jobs are projected for the future?

Click on **"See more details at O*NET Online"** at the bottom of the page for more detailed info to help answer this question.

Scroll to the bottom of the page to find "Wages & Employment Trends"

Click on "State trends"
What are the projections for your state? Select the state you wish to live in.

Employment (current)_____employees

Projected growth: _____% _____than average
Projected job openings: _____

National Trends:

Employment (current)_____employees

Projected growth: _____% _____than average

Projected job openings: _____
Analyze it: Rate your satisfaction:
Meh 1 2 3 4 5 Amazing!

Personality: Does this sound like you?
Which personality traits does your career fulfill from pages 16-18 or RIASEC on page 42 from my next move?

_____

_____

_____

Analyze it: Rate your satisfaction:
Meh 1 2 3 4 5 Amazing!

Career Values: Which career values do you think will be satisfied?

What are your top 5 career values you listed in **Step 3 from page 11**?

1)_____	Satisfied or Sacrificed?

2)_____	Satisfied or Sacrificed?

3)_____	Satisfied or Sacrificed?

4)_____	Satisfied or Sacrificed?

5)_____	Satisfied or Sacrificed?

Analyze it: Rate your satisfaction:

Meh 1 2 3 4 5 Amazing!

Evaluate it: What is your final analysis of this career. Discuss the pros and cons:

_____

_____

_____

_____

Score Career #2
Tally the satisfaction rating for each section:

Duties: ___
Knowledge: ___
Skills & Abilities: ___
Education: ___
Major: ___
Salary: ___
Outlook: ___
Personality: ___
Career Values: ___
Total: ___

Career #3 job title:_____

Are there some other titles this career may be called?
_____
_____

Daily Duties: What would you do on the job?
_____
_____
_____

Which of these duties would you enjoy the most? Are there any duties you wouldn't like?
_____
_____

Analyze it: Rate your satisfaction for how would spend your day:
             Meh 1 2 3 4 5 Amazing!

Knowledge: What would you need to study?
What would you have to study:
_____
_____

Analyze it: Rate your satisfaction:
             Meh 1 2 3 4 5 Amazing!

Skills and Abilities: What would you need to be good at?
_____
_____

Analyze it: Rate your satisfaction: Do your strengths match from pages 13-14?
             Meh 1 2 3 4 5 Amazing!

Education: How much preparation is necessary?
What are the requirements to get the job? Which level degree is necessary? example "Bachelor's Degree"

_____

What should you major in? "Google" "What should I major in to be a...?

Possible major(s): example "Accounting"

_____

_____

Analyze it: Rate your satisfaction:
Meh 1 2 3 4 5 Amazing!

Salary: What is the average salary per year?
$_____

Analyze it: Rate your satisfaction:
Meh 1 2 3 4 5 Amazing!

Click on "**See more details at O*NET Online**" at the bottom of the page for more detailed info to help answer this question.

Scroll to the bottom of the page to find "Wages & Employment Trends"

Click on "State trends"
What are the projections for your state? Select the state you wish to live in.

Employment (current)_____employees

Projected growth: _____% _____than average
Projected job openings: _____

National Trends:

Employment (current)_____employees

Projected growth: _____% _____than average

Projected job openings: _____

Analyze it: Rate your satisfaction:

Meh 1 2 3 4 5 Amazing!

Personality: Does this sound like you?

Which personality traits does your career fulfill from pages 16-18 or RIASEC on page 42 from my next move?

_____
_____
_____

Analyze it: Rate your satisfaction:

Meh 1 2 3 4 5 Amazing!

Career Values: Which career values do you think will be satisfied?

What are your top 5 career values you listed in **Step 3 from page 11**?

1)_____ Satisfied or Sacrificed?

2)_____ Satisfied or Sacrificed?

3)_____ Satisfied or Sacrificed?

4)_____ Satisfied or Sacrificed?

5)_____ Satisfied or Sacrificed?

Analyze it: Rate your satisfaction:

Meh 1 2 3 4 5 Amazing!

Evaluate it: What is your final analysis of this career. Discuss the pros and cons:

_____

_____

_____

Score Career #3
Tally the satisfaction rating for each section:

Duties: ___
Knowledge: ___
Skills & Abilities: ___
Education: ___
Major: ___
Salary: ___
Outlook: ___
Personality: ___
Career Values: ___
Total: ___

Career #4 job title:_____

Are there some other titles this career may be called?

_____

_____

Daily Duties: What would you do on the job?

_____

_____

_____

Which of these duties would you enjoy the most? Are there any duties you wouldn't like?

_____

_____

Analyze it: Rate your satisfaction for how would spend your day:

Meh 1 2 3 4 5 Amazing!

Knowledge: What would you need to study?

What would you have to study:

_____

_____

Analyze it: Rate your satisfaction:

Meh 1 2 3 4 5 Amazing!

Skills and Abilities: What would you need to be good at?

_____

_____

Analyze it: Rate your satisfaction: Do your strengths match from pages 13-14?

Meh 1 2 3 4 5 Amazing

Education: How much preparation is necessary?

What are the requirements to get the job? Which level degree is necessary? example "Bachelor's Degree"

_____

What should you major in? "Google" "What should I major in to be a…?

Possible major(s): example "Accounting"

_____

_____

Analyze it: Rate your satisfaction:

Meh 1 2 3 4 5 Amazing!

Salary: What is the average salary per year?

$_____

Analyze it: Rate your satisfaction:

Meh 1 2 3 4 5 Amazing!

Job Outlook: How many jobs are projected for the future?

Click on "**See more details at O*NET Online**" at the bottom of the page for more detailed info to help answer this question.

Scroll to the bottom of the page to find "Wages & Employment Trends"

Click on "State trends"
What are the projections for your state? Select the state you wish to live in.

Employment (current)_____employees

Projected growth: _____% _____than average
Projected job openings: _____

National Trends:

Employment (current)_____employees

Projected growth: _____% _____than average

Projected job openings: _____

Analyze it: Rate your satisfaction:
                  Meh   1   2   3   4   5   Amazing!

Personality: Does this sound like you?
Which personality traits does your career fulfill from pages 16-18 or RIASEC on page 42 from my next move?

_____

_____

_____

Analyze it: Rate your satisfaction: Meh   1   2   3   4   5   Amazing!

Career Values: Which career values do you think will be satisfied?

What are your top 5 career values you listed in **Step 3 from page 11**?

1)_____ Satisfied or Sacrificed?

2)_____ Satisfied or Sacrificed?

3)_____ Satisfied or Sacrificed?

4)_____ Satisfied or Sacrificed?

5)_____ Satisfied or Sacrificed?

Analyze it: Rate your satisfaction:

Meh 1 2 3 4 5 Amazing!

Evaluate it: What is your final analysis of this career. Discuss the pros and cons:

_____

_____

_____

_____

Score Career #4
Tally the satisfaction rating for each section:

Duties: ___
Knowledge: ___
Skills & Abilities: ___
Education: ___
Major: ___
Salary: ___
Outlook: ___
Personality: ___
Career Values: ___
Total: ___

Career #5 job title:_____

Are there some other titles this career may be called?

_____

_____

Daily Duties: What would you do on the job?

_____

_____

_____

Which of these duties would you enjoy the most? Are there any duties you wouldn't like?

_____

_____

Analyze it: Rate your satisfaction for how would spend your day:

Meh 1 2 3 4 5 Amazing!

Knowledge: What would you need to study?
What would you have to study:

_____

_____

Analyze it: Rate your satisfaction:

Meh 1 2 3 4 5 Amazing!

Skills and Abilities: What would you need to be good at?

_____

_____

Analyze it: Rate your satisfaction: Do your strengths match from pages 13-14?

Meh 1 2 3 4 5 Amazing

Education: How much preparation is necessary?
What are the requirements to get the job? Which level degree is necessary? example "Bachelor's Degree"
_____

What should you major in? "Google" "What should I major in to be a…?"

Possible major(s): example "Accounting"
_____
_____

Analyze it: Rate your satisfaction:
Meh 1 2 3 4 5 Amazing!

Salary: What is the average salary per year?
$_____

Analyze it: Rate your satisfaction:
Meh 1 2 3 4 5 Amazing!

Job Outlook: How many jobs are projected for the future?

Click on **"See more details at O*NET Online"** at the bottom of the page for more detailed info to help answer this question.

Scroll to the bottom of the page to find "Wages & Employment Trends

Click on "State trends"
What are the projections for your state? Select the state you wish to live in.

Employment (current)_____employees
Projected growth: _____% _____than average
Projected job openings: _____

National Trends:

Employment (current) _____ employees
Projected growth: _____ % _____ than average
Projected job openings: _____

Analyze it: Rate your satisfaction:

Meh 1 2 3 4 5 Amazing!

Personality: Does this sound like you?

Which personality traits does your career fulfill from pages 16-18 or RIASEC on page 42 from my next move?

_____

_____

_____

Analyze it: Rate your satisfaction:

Meh 1 2 3 4 5 Amazing!

Career Values: Which career values do you think will be satisfied?

What are your top 5 career values you listed in **Step 3 from page 11**?

1) _____   Satisfied or Sacrificed?

2) _____   Satisfied or Sacrificed?

3) _____   Satisfied or Sacrificed?

4) _____   Satisfied or Sacrificed?

5) _____   Satisfied or Sacrificed?

Analyze it: Rate your satisfaction:

Meh 1 2 3 4 5 Amazing!

Evaluate it: What is your final analysis of this career. Discuss the pros and cons:

_____

_____

_____

_____

Score Career #5
Tally the satisfaction rating for each section:

Duties: ___
Knowledge: ___
Skills & Abilities: ___
Education: ___
Major: ___
Salary: ___
Outlook: ___
Personality: ___
Career Values: ___
Total: ___

Final Analysis
Complete the satisfaction rating for each of the five careers:

1) _____ Total:___

2) _____ Total:___

3) _____ Total:___

4) _____ Total___

5) _____ Total:___

Which career has the highest score:_____

Evaluate it: Evaluate the career with the highest score.

What do you like most about it? Is there anything you dislike about it?

Pros:_____
_____
_____
_____
_____
_____
_____
_____
_____
_____
_____
_____
_____
_____

Cons:_____
_____
_____
_____
_____
_____
_____
_____

The Next Step: Job Shadow!

Research can only give you a small taste of what the career has to offer through facts and statistics. The best way to really KNOW is through your own experience.

Step 1: Find someone who does the job

- Ask your network of family and friends if they know anyone who works in the industry.

    - Example of what to say: "I am considering a career as a _____. I am interested in doing a job shadow with someone in the field to ask questions and learn more about the industry. It could be for just a couple of hours or an entire shift. Would you be able to let me job shadow you where you work?"

- If you don't know anyone, start at your local community college or university. E-mail or call instructors who teach the major and ask them if they can help you.

    - Example of what to say: "Hello, my name is _____. I am a student at _____ I am considering a career as a _____. I am interested in doing a job shadow with someone in the field to ask questions and learn more about the industry. It could be for just a couple of hours or an entire shift depending upon the person's preference. Would you be able to help me find someone who is currently working in the field to job shadow?"

- "Google" the name of your career in your city to find local companies that employ people in the industry. Example: "mechanical engineering jobs in Chicago, Illinois"

    - Call the human resource's department and tell them you would like to set up a job shadow with someone who does your career of interest.

        - Example of what to say: "Hello, my name is _____. I am a student at _____ I am considering a career as a _____. I am interested in doing a job shadow with someone in the field to ask questions and learn more about the industry. It could be for just a couple of hours or an entire shift depending upon the person's preference. Is there anyone on your staff who may be available to help me with the opportunity?"

- If you can't find anyone to job shadow in person, try to find someone to interview on the phone. Some jobs may have privacy rules or laws that prohibit in person shadows.

Step 2: Prepare questions

Make a list of questions to take with you. Be sure to write down the answers during your interview.

Suggested Questions: Choose as many from the list or your own to ask.

- On a typical day in this position, what do you do?
- What kinds of problems do you deal with? What kinds of decisions do you make?
- What part of this job do you find most satisfying? Most challenging?
- What are the personal satisfactions connected with your occupation?
- Do you find your job exciting or boring? Why?
- How does your job affect your lifestyle?
- How would you describe the atmosphere and the people with whom you work?
- Would you choose the same path for yourself if you could do things all over again? Why? What would you change?
- What personal qualities or abilities are important to success in this career?
- What is the salary range for various levels in this field?
- What are the basic prerequisites/requirements for jobs in this field? What training or education is required for this type of work?
- How well did your college experience prepare you for this job? Where did you go to school, and what did you study?
- What types of training do companies offer when entering this field? Is there on-going training?
- What are the opportunities for advancement in this field? How does a person progress within the field?
- How do you see jobs in this field changing in the future? What is the demand?
- How is the economy affecting your career?
- What special advice would you give a person entering this field?
- Which professional journals and organizations would help me learn more about this field?
- Here are some things I have done already that I think will prepare me for this career...what do you think about what I have done so far? What would you suggest further?
- How did you get your job? Can you suggest some ways a student could obtain this necessary experience?
- What entry level jobs are best for learning as much as possible?
- Do you know of any internship opportunities I could pursue?
- Who do you know that I should talk to next? When I call him/her, may I use your name?
- _____other?

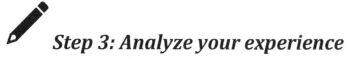

Step 3: Analyze your experience

Description: What did you do on your shadow? How did the experience make you feel?

Lessons Learned: What did you learn? What kind of requirements are there to get the job? Daily duties? Environment? What kind of career values does it satisfy? Which career values would you have to give up? Job demand? Other lessons learned…?

Opinion: Did you like or dislike the job? Why? Is this job still of interest to you after the shadow? Why or why not?

_____
_____
_____
_____
_____
_____
_____
_____
_____
_____
_____
_____
_____
_____

Step Nine: Make an Education Plan

Once you have chosen a career field, create a plan to obtain the requirements to get the job.

The Next Step: Plan a path to your career. Where will you get your education, training or experience to get the job?

In this section, you will be able to:
- ✓ Determine a Major
- ✓ Choose Type of School and Level of Education
- ✓ Identify Your Values
- ✓ Make a List of Possible Choices
- ✓ Research and Gather Data
- ✓ Analyze a Campus
- ✓ Make an Education Plan
- ✓ Research Application Requirements and Apply
- ✓ Search for Scholarships and Financial Aid
- ✓ Survive College

What do I need to be prepared and qualified?

What is a major?

Definition: A major is a field or specific subject of study.

 Consider it: Why is it important to choose a major before choosing a school?

_____

TIP: Research! Not all schools have every major! Choose the best school for YOUR necessary education!

What is your major?

What should you major in for your career? Refer to your research or google "what should I major in to be a "insert career"?

 Possible major(s):_____

Examples of possible majors:

      AGRICULTURE   **CRIMINAL JUSTICE**

      CULTURAL STUDIES   **BIOLOGY**

      COMPUTER SCIENCE   **ENGINEERING**

      EDUCATION   **JOURNALISM**

What is the **minimum** level of education for your career? Check one:

☐ *Certification/Certificate-proves qualifications based on passing specific courses or exams. Time varies from a few weeks to several months.*

☐ *Associate degree- commonly referred to a 2-year degree usually awarded by a Community College for successfully completing specific courses of 60 or more college credits.*

☐ *Bachelor's-an undergraduate degree referred to as a 4-year degree, successfully completing specific courses of 120 or more college credits at a university or college.*

☐ *Masters-a graduate degree obtaining more advanced education of a subject usually completed in 2 years after a bachelor's.*

☐ *Ph.D. (Doctorate)-a post-graduate degree is awarded to someone who has done extensive original research on a subject completing and defending a thesis or dissertation.*

☐ *Professional-after earning a bachelor's, apply to a specialized school for a professional field such as law, medical, dentistry etc. where a licensure is required.*

	Undergraduate Degree 2 or 4-year		Vocational	
	Associates	*Bachelor's*	*Certification*	*Associates*
Average Credits	60+	120+	Varies	Varies
Average Time of completion	2-3 years	4-5 years	8 weeks-2 years	18-24 months
Graduate Degree-*after* earning a Bachelor's				
	Masters	*Ph.D.*	*Professional*	
Average Credits	30+ after bachelors	120+ after bachelors	Varies based on school/degree	
Average Time of completion	1-3 years May require the GRE	3-7 years Capstone project or dissertation	2-12 years Which type of test do you need to take for admission? *Examples:* LSAT-Law School /MCAT-Medical School	

Which type of school is right for you based on your level of education required?

Check one: (use the chart below to help you)

☐ *Community*

☐ *Traditional University*

☐ *Non-Traditional University*

☐ *Vocational*

TYPES OF SCHOOLS	COMMUNITY	TRADITIONAL UNIVERSITY	NON-TRADITIONAL UNIVERSITY	VOCATIONAL
Degree	Associates, Certification	Bachelor's, Masters, PHD	*Certification, *Associates, *Bachelor's, *Masters, *PHD (*Varies from school to school)	Certification, Associates, License preparation
Tuition & Fees Averages According to College Board	$3,347	Public: $9,139 Private: $31,231	For profit: $15,160 Private: $31,231	For profit: $15,160
Education	General education and major focused	General education and major focused	Career focused, limited general education	Career focused, limited general education
Social	Some clubs, events	Numerous clubs, sports, events	Limited	Limited
Living Situation	Off-campus	On campus	Off campus	Off campus

Step 3: Identify your college values

Choose the top 5 that are important to you when choosing a college:

1) _____
2) _____
3) _____
4) _____
5) _____

- ☐ **Accreditation:** regional or nationally accredited. If you are degree seeking look for <u>regional!</u>

- ☐ **Admission criteria:** what does it take to get in: GPA, ACT/SAT scores, essay etc.?

- ☐ **Athletics:** what kinds of sports do they have?

- ☐ **Campus:** what is the environment like? Be sure to visit to see if you really like it!

- ☐ **Certifications:** are certifications offered in your skill area?

- ☐ **Career Services:** this department helps job seekers before and after graduation

- ☐ **Class size:** what is the average class size? Instructor/student ratio?

- ☐ **Clubs:** what kinds of clubs are available for your interests?

- ☐ **Degree programs/classes:** majors, programs of study, classes of interest

- ☐ **Instructor knowledge:** what kinds of backgrounds do the instructors have?

- ☐ **Internships:** short term on the job training in your career field

- ☐ **Living situation:** on-campus dorms/apartments or off-campus living

- ☐ **Location:** distance from home, job options in the city, things to do

- ☐ **Population:** how many students are in attendance/diversity

- ☐ **Religious affiliation:** does the campus meet your spirituality needs?

Continued on next page

- ☐ **Reputation:** how will this college look on your resumé?
- ☐ **Safety:** on-campus security, lighting, statistics etc.
- ☐ **Scheduling convenience:** when are classes offered: days/evening/weekend/summer?
- ☐ **Scholarships:** are there any scholarships offered specific to the college?
- ☐ **Study abroad:** study in another country for credit
- ☐ **Tuition:** cost per year or per credit hour, fees, living expenses
- ☐ **Social Events:** dances, parties, celebrations, things to do etc.

Make a List of Possible Choices

Use the College Navigator provided by the National Center for Education and Statistics: http://nces.ed.gov/collegenavigator/ ("browse programs" for your major)

College:_____
    Possible Major(s):_____
    _____
    _____

College:_____
    Possible Major(s):_____
    _____
    _____

College:_____
    Possible Major(s):_____
    _____
    _____

Step 5: Research and Gather Data for 3 Schools

Use the Big Future College Search provided by The College Board
www.bigfuture.collegeboard.org

School Name	#1	Rate your Satisfaction For all data 1-5 ⇩	#2	Rate your Satisfaction For all data 1-5 ⇩	#3	Rate your Satisfaction For all data 1-5 ⇩
Major(s) of interest						
Location (City/State)						
Student Population						
Student-to-faculty ratio						
Tuition & Fees	$		$		$	
Cost of room & board	$		$		$	
ACT/SAT Mid-Range Score						
Important admission factors						
Student Life: Clubs, etc.						
Athletics						
Other?						
Final total:		Total:____		Total:____		Total:____

Analyze a Campus -Visit

Always visit the college campus no matter what type of college or how far away. It is important to get a feel for where you be getting your education and if it is right for you.

College Name:_____

Career:_____

Do they have your major (s) :_____

_____

_____

Type of school: Traditional   Non-Traditional   Community   Trade/vocational

- Is this the right type of school for your career path? **Yes/No**

Desired Cost: 10,000 or less per year $20,000 or less per year $30,000 or less per year

$40,000 or less per year $50,000 or less per year   more than $50,000 per year

- How well does the cost of tuition meet your needs: **NOT-** 1   2   3   4   5 **Perfect**

Admission Requirements: SAT/ACT:_____**GPA:**_____**Essay: Y/N**

- How do you feel about the admission requirements: **NOT-** 1   2   3   4   5 **Perfect**

School Reputation: **NOT-**1   2   3   4   5 **Perfect**

Reputation for your major: **NOT-**1   2   3   4   5 **Perfect**

Location: City   Rural   close to home   far from home

What kinds of businesses or activities would you like have near campus?

_____   _____   _____

_____   _____   _____

- How well does the location meet your needs: **NOT-**1   2   3   4   5 **Perfect**

Environment Size: Small   Medium   Large

- How well does the size meet your needs: **NOT**-1 2 3   4   5 **Perfect**

Athletics desired:_____

- How well do the athletics offered meet your needs: **NOT**-1   2 3   4   5 **Perfect**

Living needs:_____

- How well does the living situation meet your needs: **NOT**-1   2   3   4   5 **Perfect**

Food options:

- How well do the food options meet your needs: **NOT**-1   2   3   4   5 **Perfect**

Extracurricular desires:_____

                             _____

                             _____

- How well do the extra-curricular meet your needs: **NOT**-1 2 3   4   5 **Perfect**

Resources desired: Labs   Library   Tutoring   other:_____

- How well do the resources meet your needs: **NOT**-1   2 3   4   5 **Perfect**

Students:

- How well will you fit in with the student body: **NOT**-1   2 3   4   5 **Perfect**

Teachers:

- How do you like the teachers (may need to do this on a separate visit for your major specifically)
  NOT-1   2 3   4   5 **Perfect**

Evaluate it: I am considering/not considering this school because of the following pros and cons

_____

_____

_____

Step 7: Create Your Education Plan

What is your ideal career:_____

What can you major in:_____

Which level of degree do you need:_____

Which type of school is needed:_____

Plan your pathway: (all boxes do NOT have to be completed)

level of degree + level of degree + level of degree + level of degree
College:_____ College:_____ College:_____ College:_____

Example:

| Associate of Science General | Bachelor of Science Computer Science | Master of Science Computer Science | PH. D Doctor of Computer Science |

level of degree + level of degree + level of degree + level of degree
College: *Pikes Peak Community*   College: *UCCS*   College: *UCCS*   College: *UCCS*

ACTIVITY: Print out your degree plan to use as a guide

❖ Print the list of courses you need to obtain your Associate and/or Bachelor Degree from your school of choice for your desired major

> *Many students will begin at a community college and then transfer to complete their education at a university. It is important to investigate which credits will transfer to complete your degree requirements.*

To find a list for your degree requirements from your school of choice:

➢ Go to the school's website and search: "Academics" "Degree Programs", or "Undergraduate Degrees", or Majors/programs".

***TIP:* Be patient.** It may take a lot of searching to find the list of classes for your major. Some websites are not very user friendly. E-mail or call the academic advising department if you are unable to find it on the website. <u>Don't give up!</u>

Example: This is an example plan used for advising. It may be a 4-year plan or a simple list of courses

Use this list as a map and communicate with an advisor

Step 8: Research Application Requirements and Apply

Admissions Standards Based on Type of School

TYPES OF SCHOOLS	COMMUNITY	TRADITIONAL UNIVERSITY	NON-TRADITIONAL UNIVERSITY	VOCATIONAL
Admissions Standards	Open Admissions	No Set Standards/competitive	*Open Admissions (*May vary from school to school)	Open Admissions

Note: Some traditional universities have open admission depending on the state policy

Open Admissions: admission policy that does not require specified standards except a high school diploma.

No Set Standards/ Competitive: Set of admission requirements specified by college which may include:

- GPA, Class rank, HEAR requirements, ACT/ SAT, essay, recommendations, extra-curricular activities etc.

WARNING: be realistic when it comes to application requirements. Be sure your GPA and test scores align with your school choice. If your academic performance suffered in high school, go to a community college first to start fresh. If you perform well, then apply to a university.

HEAR Requirements: Higher Education Admission Requirements

Higher Education Admission Requirements vary by state.

Be sure to research your state's policies!

General education courses that must be taken in high school to be considered admission to a traditional university.

Example from State of Colorado

Academic Area Completed in High School	2010+ High School Graduates
English	4 years
Mathematics (3 years must include Algebra I, Geometry, Algebra II, or equivalents)	4 years
Natural/Physical Science (2 years must be lab based)	3 years
Social Sciences (At least one year must be US or World History)	3 years
Foreign Language	1 year(note: many require 2)
Academic electives	2 years

[9]Source: Colorado Department of Higher Education.

---

[9] "Higher Education Admission Requirements," *Colorado Department of Higher Education*, July 2022, Higher Education Admission Recommendations | Higher Education (colorado.gov)

Find out if you need to get letters of recommendation or write an admission essay

Letters of recommendation

<u>Only</u> ask for a letter of recommendation when required by your college or scholarship!

What to give your teacher/advisor/counselor when requesting a letter of recommendation:

1) An envelope addressed to the college with a stamp ready to mail or e-mail online link

2) Provide information about what values or criteria the college/scholarship is looking for

3) Ask <u>WAY</u> in advance (at least 1 month) and provide due date

4) Get a recommendation packet from advisor/counselor or bring a resumé detailing your accomplishments

5) Write a thank you card!!!

Admissions essays/personal statements

Why do they want me to write an essay?

- Helps college reps or scholarship committees see you as a person outside of your academics

Tips:

- Spell Check and proofread!!!
- Write with emotion and passion and be yourself!
- Meet the required length, If the requirements state 650 words, <u>do not</u> exceed the word count!

How do I know what to write about?

- Usually there will be a required essay prompt or a choice of prompts

   Example: "Discuss an obstacle you have faced or problem you have solved. What were the steps you took to be successful? What did you learn about yourself in the process?"

Standardized Tests-Find out which <u>may</u> be required for your college admission

Test	ACT	PSAT	SAT
When	Spring Junior Year	Sophomore Year	Junior/Senior Year
Score range	1-36 Composite score=average of tests	160-760 each test Added together total=320-1520	400-1600
Subjects	English, Math, Reading, Science	Reading, Writing, Language, Math	Reading, Writing, Language, Math
Website	www.act.org	www.collegeboard.org	www.collegeboard.org

<u>Where</u> do I apply to college?

1) The Common Application: www.commonapp.org is a great place to apply with over 700 colleges to choose from. Simply complete one application, up load your admission essay, and select which colleges to send it to. It is also a great resource to research colleges and admission requirements.

2) You can also apply under the "admissions" tab on your college's website.

<u>When</u> should I apply to college?

 ACTIVITY: Research admission requirements and deadlines.

Many traditional universities' <u>deadline</u> is March 1st of your senior year.

College	#1	#2	#3
Deadline to Apply			
Financial Aid Deadline			
Scholarship Deadline			
Recommendation required?			
GPA range			
Essay Required Y/N			

Step 9: Search for Scholarships and Financial Aid

Check out these scholarship search engines. All are <u>free</u> and private.

Careeronestop.org (search scholarship finder) Fastweb.org Scholarships.com Collegenet.com

- Name of scholarship_____
- When should you apply?_____
- What do you have to do?_____
- How much $?_____
- Where do you apply?_____

- Name of scholarship_____
- When should you apply?_____
- What do you have to do?_____
- How much $?_____
- Where do you apply?_____

- Name of scholarship_____
- When should you apply?_____
- What do you have to do?_____
- How much $?_____
- Where do you apply?_____

- Name of scholarship_____
- When should you apply?_____
- What do you have to do?_____
- How much $?_____
- Where do you apply?_____

- Name of scholarship_____
- When should you apply?_____
- What do you have to do?_____
- How much $?_____
- Where do you apply?_____

Automatic Scholarships

Some colleges give automatic scholarships based on SAT/ACT scores, as well as qualifiers like GPA or class rank. **For these scholarships, you don't have to submit any extra application information, but in some cases, you should apply by a certain deadline to be guaranteed the scholarship.** Be sure to check out each college's website.

Apply for Financial Aid

There are tons of acronyms and terms that can lead to confusion. Let's make this step simple!

What is the FAFSA?

The FAFSA is the *Free Application for Federal Student Aid*. It is an online form that will determine your eligibility for financial aid to pay for college. Go to https://fafsa.gov *to apply.* All students should apply each year.

TIP: Financial aid is always FREE! You should <u>never</u> be asked to pay any fees when applying.
Be sure to use the website: https://fafsa.gov *to apply.*
For FAQ go to https://studentaid.ed.gov/sa/

---

[10]*What kind of aid could I get?*

Grants- FREE federal $ you won't have to pay back. This $ is based on financial need.

Loans- There are two types of loans: federal and private. Both are *borrowed* $ and must be paid back!

    Federal loans are provided by the federal government. They will generally have lower interest, no credit check is necessary, you will not get a bill until you leave college or drop below ½ time status, and may offer personalized repayment plans. Also, a subsidized loan does not accrue interest while in school.

    Private loans are provided by a bank, other financial institution, or a school. These are usually higher interest and less benefits.

Work study jobs- A part-time job to help pay for school expenses for students with a financial need. The job may be working on campus or for a nonprofit organization benefiting the public.

Every little bit helps! Use all your resources to chip away at tuition.

---

[10]"Types of Aid," *Federal Student* Aid: *Office of the U.S. Department of Education,*
https://studentaid.ed.gov/sa/types.

What is aid based on?

Aid is awarded to undergraduate students with financial need based on your parent's income as a dependent student. You are no longer considered a dependent after you are 24 years old, get married, have a child of your own, and other possible factors. Go to https://studentaid.ed.gov/sa/sites/default/files/2017-18-efc-formula.pdf for a detailed list of what defines an "independent" student.

[11]Financial need is determined by the difference between the cost of attendance (COA) and your expected family contribution (EFC). The COA is made up of tuition, fees, and other expenses for school. The EFC is an index number your school will use to decide how much aid you will get if you go to their school.

Use the FAFSA4caster as a planning tool to help estimate your federal aid and create strategies to pay for college. https://studentaid.ed.gov/sa/fafsa/estimate

---

When do I apply?

Apply as early as October1st your senior year and each year thereafter while in college. Deadlines may vary by state and **most colleges have their own deadlines much sooner than June 30th.**

What happens after I apply?

Three days to three weeks later you will get a Student Aid Report (SAR) which is a summary of your data. Review the summary to ensure it is accurate.

After that, the school you applied to will send you an award letter stating how much aid you will get if you attend their school.

If you have questions or need support, contact the financial aid office at the college.

---

[11] https://studentaid.ed.gov/sa/fafsa/next-steps/how-calculated

Survive College

There are a few key elements to surviving college and reaching your goals. In this section, you will be able to:

- ✓ Manage your time
- ✓ Use learning strategies
- ✓ Self-advocate

Manage Your Time

Managing time and beating procrastination is a constant struggle for most people. It is important to embrace some time management tools to accomplish goals both big and small. It will also help conquer stress.

 Evaluate it: How are you doing with your time management?

Most of the time I...	Well	Could improve
use a planner or calendar		
create "to do lists"		
stay organized		
prioritize		
celebrate accomplishments		
leave extra time if problems arise		

 Analyze it: How do you think you could improve your time management?

Time Management Strategies

#1 Use a "To Do" List

I love to use "to do" lists! Here's why:

- I brain-dump everything that is on my mind so I can STOP thinking about it and START doing it.

- Checking things off the list makes me feel like I have accomplished something.

- I actually get things done!

3 easy steps to make an effective "to do" list:

1) **Brain-dump**-list everything you need to do in no apparent order

2) **Estimate time**- roughly estimate how much time each task will take. This will help with step 3 if you need to chunk up a task.

3) **Prioritize**-decide what is the most important to do today. I like to simply circle or star my main priorities. Don't choose more than 3-5. Then put in order of which one will go first. Stick with what you need to work on. I love to procrastinate by doing everything on my to do list EXCEPT the one thing I know I should be doing. Commit!

   Example:

    • 5-page paper for English (2-3 hours)

    • Daily Math problems (20 minutes)

   - Do laundry (2 hours)

   - Reading/notes for History pages 30-55 (1 hour)

   - Study for science test (30 minutes each)

Apply it: Make a to do list using the 3 steps (brain-dump, estimate time, prioritize)

_____

_____

_____

_____

_____

#2 Use a Planning Tool

Use a tool that *works* for *YOU!*

Choose a planner, phone, or calendar etc.

The most common complaint I hear about using a planner is "I never look at it so why bother?" Make it your best friend and it will never let you down!

NAME YOUR PLANNER!

YOU ARE LESS LIKELY TO NEGLECT IT.

My planner's name is: _____

Using your planning tool:

1) Fill in deadlines as soon as you know them

2) Use reminders (set reminders on your phone, use sticky notes etc.)

#3 Practice Backward Planning

Start with deadlines then plan when you will the complete chunks to meet the deadline.

My to do list for the week:

- 5-page paper for English
- Daily Math problems
- Do laundry
- Reading for History pages 30-55
- Take out the garbage
- Movie with friends
- Science test

> *1) Make a to do list*
> *2) Write in deadlines*
> *3) Plan chunks to meet deadline*

TIP! USE DIFFERENT COLOR CATEGORIES

HIGHLIGHT DEADLINES!!!

Monday	Tuesday	Wednesday	Thursday	Friday	Saturday	Sunday
Format paper- choose topic Math odds	Math odds Reading for History pages 30-40	Math odds Paper outline Reading for History pages 41-55	Math odds Review for Math test (30 minutes)	Math quiz Work on 1st draft -finish at least 2 pages	Sleep in! Do laundry & work on 1st draft -finish at least 2 pages Movie 7pm	Work on final draft Make Science flash cards Garbage
Monday	**Tuesday**	**Wednesday**	**Thursday**	**Friday**	**Saturday**	**Sunday**
Math odds Science flash cards	Math odds Science flash cards	Math odds **English Paper due** Science flash cards	Math odds Science flash cards	**Science Test**	Sleep in! Babysit 6pm	Garbage

Set goals for accomplishments

Decide how much time you will spend on each item or set a goal for a chunk of what you want to accomplish. This helps reduce stress to get it done.

As seen above, I have planned chunks of my English paper to get it done before the due date. I have also planned how much time I will commit to studying for the Science test.

Set a goal and you will feel accomplished!

Attack "Time Stealers!"

A time stealer is something unplanned that uses your time.

Examples: social media, taking care of a sibling, video games, traffic, even homework!

Consider it: What steals your time?

_____

_____

Get Rid of "Time Stealers!"

Options:

1) Plan time for it-be realistic about how much time it takes

2) Get rid of it! Or limit it.   - it takes 21 days to make a habit!

Apply it: What are you going to do about YOUR time stealers?

_____

_____

PROCRASTINATION

I love to procrastinate! It is so much easier to do something you WANT to do rather than something you MUST do.

However, there are reasons *why* we procrastinate.

Students say they procrastinate because:

- They have too much to do and feel overwhelmed
- Don't feel like doing it right now
- Fear of failure
- Fear of success, leading to higher expectations
- Not knowing where to start
- Being unorganized
- Perfectionism-if I can't do it perfect right now, I will wait until I can
- No motivation

☐ NOW

☒ LATER

Analyze it: Why do YOU procrastinate? Come on, I know you do!

_____

_____

_____

How to beat procrastination:

- Stop thinking about it and just start it
- Make a to do list
- Prioritize
- Do it in chunks
- Set goals with realistic times of completion
- Change up what you're working on
- Celebrate each accomplishment
- Find meaning in everything you do

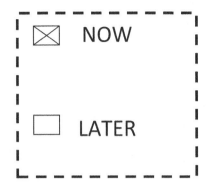

Apply it: What can <u>you</u> do to beat procrastination?

_____

_____

_____

_____

Use Learning Strategies

To reach goals it is essential to learn something new. Whether it is for school, a job, or a new skill, learning will need to take place. Students are especially guilty of "learn and purge" (memorizing something long enough to take a test.) To do something well it is important to "learn" it especially if it's needed for your job.

Evaluate it: How are you doing with your study habits?

Most of the time I...	Well	Could improve
Take quality notes		
Review notes within 24 hours		
Create a study guide		
Use flashcards		
Study in a group		
Use memory strategies		
Plan time to study		

Apply it: What can you do to improve your study habits?

_____

_____

_____

[12]A University of Texas study found that MOST people remember:
- 10 percent of what they read
- 20 percent of what they hear
- 30 percent of what they see
- 50 percent of what they see and hear
- 70 percent of what they say
- 90 percent of what they do and say

How do we learn?

[13]Learning something physically changes the brain, nerve cells make new connections between neurons called synapses:

- The more you learn the more connections you make

- The more you practice the stronger the connection/memory becomes just like a muscle gets stronger by lifting weights

- The cells organize themselves into groups that specialize in different kinds of information processing

- To be converted from short-term to long-term memory repetition is necessary. Hence why we practice and STUDY.

---

[12] T. Metcalf, "Listening to Your Clients, Life Association News 92, no. 7 (1997): 16-18

[13] Richard C. Mohs, "How Human Memory Works," *HowStuffWorks.com*. May 8, 2007, http://science.howstuffworks.com/life/inside-the-mind/human-brain/human-memory.htm.

Use the 4 rules of studying:

1. **M**anage information
2. **U**se your senses
3. **S**chedule time
4. **T**ools-utilize study tools

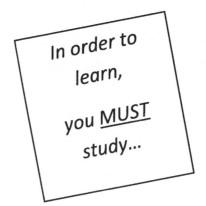
In order to learn, you MUST study...

The key to learning is making information brain friendly!

1. Manage information

Decide "WHAT" exactly needs to be studied, FOCUS on what to remember!

LEARNING TAKES <u>FOCUS</u>

- Take good notes! Listen for cues during class of what is important
- Use end of chapter questions, quizzes
- Define vocabulary terms
- Pay attention to review and repetition in class

Rules for taking quality notes:

- ☐ Don't write in complete sentences
- ☐ Summarize and condense information
- ☐ Write in your own words
- ☐ Use consistent formatting
- ☐ Skip lines in between sub-topics
- ☐ Clearly identify key points (bold, color, or underlined)
- ☐ Use good details to support the main idea

TIP: Watch a YouTube on how to take notes for a tutorial!

Use your notes to create a study guide

WHY?
A study guide condenses the most important information to study
It will help you predict exam questions
Rewriting the important points will help you remember

5 steps to creating a study guide:

1. **Gather** all the notes/info needed
2. **Condense** using the most important info
3. Highlight **key words** or phrases
4. Create quiz **questions** and compose the answers next to or under the question
5. **Add memory strategies:** color, pictures and mnemonic devices

> Be sure to include important vocabulary terms!

Example:

Question:	Answer:
What are the 5 steps to making a study guide?	1. <u>G</u>ather notes
	2. <u>C</u>ondense important info
	3. Highlight <u>k</u>ey words
	4. Predict test <u>q</u>uestions
	5. <u>A</u>dd memory strategies
	Memory Strategy: Acrostic
	<u>G</u>ood <u>c</u>hildren <u>k</u>eep <u>q</u>uiet <u>a</u>lways

2. Use your senses

- Visual: Use your eyes and imagination
    - Use color, videos, diagrams, mind maps etc.
- Auditory: Listen and speak
    - Teach it to someone else
    - Study with a group
    - Read out loud
- Movement: Hands-on use
    - Writing notes
    - Creating study guides or flash cards
    - Practicing and applying

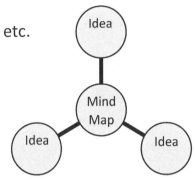

> **While many students tend to like using one sense more than another, the more senses that are combined, the more deeply it will be learned.**

3. Schedule time

Study for several short sessions instead of cramming. Schedule 30-60-minute blocks time in your planner to study for 3-5 days.

Think of your brain making memory like building a muscle, it gets stronger over time by exercising each day.

Monday	Tuesday	Wednesday	Thursday	Friday	Saturday
Review notes Make flash cards 45 min	Study flashcards 30 min	Study flashcards 30 min	Study most difficult set of questions 30 min	TEST!!!	Sleep in!

Sleep!

Don't stay up all night studying!

During REM sleep your brain processes information you learned.

4. Study tools

Use mnemonic devices

- Acronyms: Make a word from the 1st letters

    > "Parentheses, Exponents, Multiplication and Division, and Addition and Subtraction".

    Example: PEMDAS

✏️ **Apply it:** Create an acronym for the 3 steps to making a "to do list":   _____ **Brain-dump/Estimate time/Prioritize**

- Acrostics: Make a sentence from an acronym

    Example: (PEMDAS) = "Please excuse my dear aunt sally"

✏️ **Apply it:** Create an acrostic from your "to do" list:_____

Tip: "google" mnemonic devices to get ideas to help you:

For example, you are struggling with the order of the algorithm of a long division problem look up: "algorithm of a long division mnemonic"

Example: Does McDonalds Sell Cheese Burgers?
DMSCBS stands for **divide, multiply, subtract, check** that the divisor is larger than your remainder, **bring** down the next number and **start** all over again.

Loci or mind palace

- Learning a list of items in order by associating them to physical locations.

- Back in the old days politicians used this method to remember key points of their speech by associating points with objects they could see from the stage in order.

    - You could do this with items in your bedroom to remember the order of anything you are learning.

    OR

    - Create a story where each word or idea you must remember cues the next idea you need to recall.

    - *Example:* If you had to remember the words focus, written, plan, and smart to learn the 4 rules of goal setting you could invent a story about a detective that had to <u>focus</u> a magnifying glass to look at <u>writing</u> on a paper which turns out to be the villain's <u>plan.</u> The detective out "<u>smarts</u>" the villain.

TIP: there are some cool tutorials on YouTube for how to use the "mind palace."

Flash cards or free online study tools:

Quizlet, Khan Academy, Tiny Cards

- Use these on your phone or PC to create games, practice tests and more for FREE!
- Crash Course on YouTube also has some amazing tutorials!

> *татр: Use your flashcards or app during "empty time" like riding the bus or waiting in line.*

Study Groups

It is much more fun to study with others and uses your senses!

Teach it to someone else!
#1 learning strategy

1. **Invite 2-3 people** who study and won't get off topic

2. **Choose a good spot to study:** Choose a quiet place to study like the library, bookstore or coffee shop. If you choose someone's home, be sure to have a designated place without distractions

3. **Make a pact to focus:** silence cell phones, plan a block of time to focus, complete your assigned role in advance to be prepared for the session

4. **Designate roles:**

    1. Group leader: the leader will choose the study format, time block, and begin and start the session

    2. Time manager: keep time to take breaks and pace so the group doesn't get stuck on one section or topic too long

    3. Snack leader: assign someone to bring tasty snacks and drinks. Rotate this role

5. **Choose a study format**

    Options:

    1. Assign everyone a section of notes or textbook and get together to teach the material to the rest of the group

    2. Assign each person a section to teach to everyone to make a combined study guide or flash cards

    3. Quiz each other using study guides, pre-made practice tests or questions, or flash cards

Self-advocate

This may be the most important your success.

If you don't ask, you don't get. What's the worst that could happen?

> "I've never found anybody that didn't want to help me if I asked for help. Most people never ask, and that's what separates the people that do things from the people that just dream about them."
>
> Steve Jobs

Ask for help!

Whether you are asking for help or resolving a problem, these steps will help:

Step 1: Cool Down: take a step back and identify your problem. Set up a private meeting to discuss the issue.

Step 2: Clarify: calmly let the person know what you need by being specific.

Do not place blame by using an "I statement".

When ... Describe the behavior you are reacting to in a non-blameful, and non-judgmental manner. _Don't use absolutes!_

I feel ... Say how you feel. (This is the important part to prevent a buildup of feelings.)

I'd prefer ... Tell the person what you want or what the preferred action would be.

Example: When I don't get enough help in class, I feel lost. I'd prefer to get more help so I understand the material better."

Step 3: Consider- brainstorm possible solutions by asking for their ideas and giving yours

Step 4: Choose-agree on a solution by restating <u>what</u> will happen AND <u>when</u>

Step 5: Carry out-follow through with the solution and evaluate how well it worked for future issues

Sending an e-mail

You wouldn't believe some of the un-professional e-mails that I have received! Make a good impression with your teacher and others.

Follow these guidelines:

- Use a specific subject line and leave out confidential/sensitive info (others may see it)
- Use Mr./Mrs. To be respectful
- Get to the point! Make it short or nobody will read it.
- Organize your thoughts, is it clear?
- Do not abbreviate, this is not a text message
- Do not go into detail about personal or family issues
- Proofread
- Do not use slang
- Sign off: respectfully, thank you, best, with appreciation
- Use your first, last name, class name, and period

Most teachers are really good about e-mail communication and will get back to you ASAP.

TIP: <u>Be proactive!!!</u> Use e-mail if you are going to be absent or if you have questions about an upcoming assignment.

Example:

Mrs. Smith,
I will not be able to attend class tomorrow due to illness. I will be sure to get notes from a classmate. I would greatly appreciate any assigned work I missed so I do not fall behind.

Thank you,

First and last name, class name

Step Ten: Get the Job

Whether you are looking or a part-time job, an internship or a career, the steps to getting a job are all very similar.

You will be able to:
- ✓ Step 1 Consider what employers want
- ✓ Step 2 List your experience
- ✓ Step 3 Identify your top qualities and skills
- ✓ Step 4 Find a position that suits you
- ✓ Step 5 Apply for a job
- ✓ Step 6 Compose a resumé and cover letter
- ✓ Step 7 Follow interview standards
- ✓ Step 8 Formulate answers to typical interview questions

Three Golden Rules to Getting a Job

1) Tailor your qualities and skills to the job duties in your application, resumé, and interview

2) It is not what the company can do for you, but what you can do for the company

3) Focus on your strengths, leave out the negatives.

> PUT YOURSELF IN THE SHOES OF THE HIRING MANAGER OR ORGANIZATION LEADER. THEY WANT TO HIRE SOMEONE WHO ADDS VALUE TO THE COMPANY. IF YOU DO NOT ADD VALUE, THEY WILL FIND SOMEONE ELSE WHO WILL.

Step One: Consider it, what do employers want?

To get hired, it is your job to communicate that you have the qualities and skills employers are looking for. No matter who you ask or what you read about what employers want, they all consistently say the same things.

Employers want:

- A strong work ethic
- Leadership abilities
- Team work
- Communication skills
- Problem solving
- Computer skills
- Analytical skills
- Adaptability
- Initiative
- Planning and prioritizing work

Which of these are your strengths right now?

How can you prove that you have these skills?

<u>Don't worry</u> you will have more experience in college and part-time jobs that will help you develop these!

Step Two: List experience that demonstrates your qualities and skills

What have you done? Have you had an official part-time or full-time job? Have you babysat regularly? Have you volunteered for your church or local organization? Do you belong to a club, team, or leadership organization in or outside of school?

Most Valuable!!! Start with paid positions: _____

_____

2nd Most Valuable!!! List any volunteer work: _____

_____

School or extra-curricular experience: _____

_____

The BEST way to gain experience is to volunteer and work for free!!!!

Step Three: Identify the qualities and skills you gained from experience

ACTIVITY: Circle <u>your</u> top qualities and skills:

adaptability	polite	maturity	trustworthiness
commitment	positive attitude	organization	typing
communication	patience	phone	versatile
skills-oral or written	interpersonal skills	communication	willingness to learn
computer software	independence	self-motivated	mature
conflict resolution	integrity	neat appearance	proactive
customer service	intelligence	problem solving	
detail-oriented	knowledgeable	respectful	
dependability	leadership	enthusiastic	
follow/give	logical	strong work ethic	
directions	math/money	team work	

ACTIVITY: Put it all together!

Be able to explain how you have demonstrated your strengths through experience:

What would you say if a hiring manager said," tell me about a time when you have demonstrated (quality/skill)."

Example:

Position/title: _____Team Member_____

What skills did you demonstrate through responsibilities?

"I demonstrated attention to detail, team work and communication by communicating with the back of the house to ensure orders were made to customer specifications in a timely manner."

Position/title: _____

What skills did you demonstrate through responsibilities?

_____
_____
_____
_____

Position/title: _____

What skills did you demonstrate through responsibilities?

_____
_____
_____
_____

Step Four: *Find a position that suits YOU!*

✏️ ACTIVITY: *What are you looking for?*

- ❖ Describe your ideal responsibilities, what would you do?_____
  _____
  Examples: Manage, organize, data entry, customer service, office, food service

- ❖ What type of schedule/shift are you looking for?
  _____

- ❖ Does the company offer benefits, scholarships etc.?

- ❖ What is your desired environment? _____ *Examples:* High energy, people oriented, independent, professional, retail, food service, etc.

Where?

- ❖ Network! Talk to people you know. Tell them you are looking for a position.

- ❖ Search websites: www.indeed.com www.snagajob.com www.careerbuilder.com

- ❖ If searching for a part-time job, go to the places you frequent. You already have an interest in these places, why not work there? Apply!

List a few positions that interest you:

1. _____
2. _____
3. _____

ACTIVITY: *Search for a job*

1) Go to www.indeed.com, www.snagajob.com, or www.careerbuilder.com

2) Search for a specific job title or keywords in the city you live in.

3) Click on an open position you want to explore and read the job description.

4) List key words that you like in the job description:

   ➢ _____
   ➢ _____
   ➢ _____
   ➢ _____
   ➢ _____
   ➢ _____

Which kinds of qualities do you think the employer is looking for based on the job description?

   ➢ _____
   ➢ _____
   ➢ _____
   ➢ _____
   ➢ _____

Do you have these qualities? If so, apply!

Step Five: *Apply for a job*

Rules for filling out an application

- **Dress nicely if requesting an application in person**.

- **Talk with the person** who gives you the application and introduce yourself (Be sure to drop in when it isn't busy!).

- **Complete all requested information.** Don't leave anything blank. If you don't know the details, bring the application home and return it when it's completed.

- **Write clearly and neatly**, using black or blue ink.

- **Check for spelling and grammatical errors.** Proofread your job application!

- **List your most recent and relevant job first.**

- **List your most recent education first.** ONLY list the school you currently attend or have earned a diploma or degree.

- **References:**

    - Coaches, teachers, organizations where you have volunteered.

    - In all cases, ask for permission prior to using the person for a reference.

- **Don't forget to sign your application**

Tip: Be sure to include specific key words from the job description especially when applying online to survive the screening!

Compose a resumé and cover letter

A resumé is a snapshot of your qualifications for the position. Make it simple and specific.

Rules for writing a resumé

- **Tailor it to the job!** Every time you apply for a different position, you should tweak your resumé to fit the position by using the most relevant skills and experience.

- Use a template on Word or another program

- Use font that's easy to read

- Use plain white paper

- Limit to 1 page, it should be brief and to the point

- Don't use complete sentences, use bullets

- List most recent experience to past

- Proofread more than once by more than one person

Steps to write your resumé:

1. Choose template to fit your experience

    - **Functional**-you have little or no official experience. In this type of template, you will focus on proving your qualities and skills through a variety of unofficial job history.

    OR

    - **Chronological**-you have had 2-3 jobs and are able to demonstrate your qualities and skills though your duties on the job and long-term work history.

> To find a template on Word: go to "file", "new", then search for functional or chronological resumé. Fill in your information following the rules.

2. Select a position and company to apply

3. Create a summary statement on your resumé if you have some experience in your field or an objective statement if you lack official experience.

Objective Statement

Seeking a position as a(n)_____in a _____(environment) where I may utilize my _____(relevant quality) and _____(relevant skill).

Example:

- Seeking a position as a team member in a fast-paced restaurant where I may utilize my positive attitude and customer service experience to provide a quality customer experience.

- Use **key words** you find in the job ad to match what they want. Example: "positive attitude"

> *The summary is the MOST important part of your resumé!!! It is an attention getter that tells the employer exactly WHY you are qualified.*

4. Choose experience or qualities/skills that would be desired in the job you are applying for

5. Write concise bulleted sections with descriptions about your experience. Begin with a past tense verb

    - *Use the list on the following page to help diversify your verbs*

6. Find good references who are NOT family members or personal friends and ask them to be a reference. Past supervisors, teachers, coaches, and family friends are good references.

Use the verbs below to help you describe your experience

achieved
adapted
administered
advanced
advised
approved
assembled
attained
balanced
began
broadened
budgeted
built
calculated
catalogued
clarified
composed
communicated
conceived
conducted
connected
constructed
completed
compiled
composed
consulted
coordinated
created
demonstrated
designed
developed
directed
enforced
engineered
enhanced
enlarged
ensured

established
estimated
evaluated
examined
executed
extended
facilitated
financed
finished
founded
generated
grew
guided
identified
illustrated
implemented
improved
increased
installed
integrated
initiated
interpreted
interviewed
introduced
launched
lead
led
maintained
managed
maximized
monitored
motivated
negotiated
nurtured
opened
operated
organized
participated
perfected
piloted
planned

produced
programmed
proposed
provided
qualified
researched
reduced
refined
reinforced
revamped
reviewed
revised
scheduled
served
set
simplified
solved
started
streamlined
succeeded
supervised
taught
trained
upgraded
verified
wrote

Amazing Student

DO NOT INCLUDE YOUR ADDRESS | Cell: (123) 999-3337 | firstname.lastname@mail.com

Summary
Enthusiastic and detailed receptionist with a passion for customer service. Experience in a fast paced and professional environment using my positive attitude and organization to provide a quality customer experience.

Education

My High School | Diploma May 27, 2025
- GPA 3.5

Concurrently Enrolled | My Town Community College
- Completed 25 credit hours toward A.S. degree

Student Council | August 2020 – Present
- Organize and promote school events by working as a team
- Sold tickets and made change for sales
- Elected Secretary through showing attention to detail

> *This is a "chronological" style resume. It is useful for students who have some experience.*

Experience

Receptionist | My Hair Salon | October 2020 – January 2021
- Answer phones with professional greeting
- Make accurate appointments for clients

Customer Service Representative | Mail Order Catalog | October 2020 – January 2021
- Took mail-in and phone orders in a fast-paced environment
- Completed data entry for sales with attention to detail
- Used problem solving and conflict resolution to handle customer complaints and questions

Achievements
- Promoted to orange belt Jiu Jitsu Academy

[phone]•[e-mail]

Amazing Student

> *This is a "functional" style resume. It is useful for students who have very little experience to highlight strengths.*

Summary

Seeking a position as a cashier in a customer-oriented environment where I may utilize my people skills and strong work ethic.

Qualifications

Responsible (example)

- Maintained perfect attendance record for classes and school events
- Handled money for ticket sales for school dances
- Cared for two children ages 2 and 5 while maintaining and fun and safe environment

Quality or Skill

- Example of how you have demonstrated that skill or quality-begin with a past tense verb
- Example of how you have demonstrated that skill or quality-begin with a past tense verb
- Example of how you have demonstrated that skill or quality-begin with a past tense verb

Quality or Skill

- Example of how you have demonstrated that skill or quality-begin with a past tense verb
- Example of how you have demonstrated that skill or quality-begin with a past tense verb
- Example of how you have demonstrated that skill or quality-begin with a past tense verb

Education

| Name of your High School | High School | May, 2020 |

References (if you have nothing else, list references to fill the page)

Name	Who they are to you	Phone #
Kristi Smith	Teacher	(555) 444-0000

Amazing Student
888-812-6114
Amazing.student@e-mail.com

Noodles and Company
5166 N. Amazing Avenue
City, State 80007

> Use a cover letter to accompany your resume. It gives you a chance to explain why you are interested and qualified for the position. It will help you stand out when done correctly.

August 16th 2022

Dear Hiring Manager,

I am interested in the Team Member position at the Noodles and Company advertised online.

I have excellent communication skills and an aptitude for customer service. My past experience as a Customer Service Representative gave me experience working in a team, taking orders, and providing quality customer service. I believe this experience has prepared me to be a valued member of the team at Noodles and Company.

I want to work at Noodles and Company because it is a unique restaurant. I always feel welcome and enjoy trying new food on the menu each time I visit. I believe that my communication skills, customer service abilities, and positive work ethic would make me an asset to your team.

Thank you for your consideration. I look forward to meeting with you to discuss the opportunity. I can be reached at 888-812-6114.

Sincerely,

Amazing Student

Follow up after applying

Keep track of where you applied

Company Name	Position	Date of application	Contact person	Contact information (phone/e-mail)

Follow-up script

Call to follow up a few days to one week after submitting your application.

"Hello, my name is_____I submitted my application for your __ position last week, and I just wanted to make sure you received my application. I am very interested in the position and would like to set up a time schedule an interview."

Thank you for your consideration and I look forward to meeting with you soon.

Preparing for the interview checklist:

- ✓ Research the company
- ✓ Research the job description for the position
- ✓ Prepare answers for typical interview questions
- ✓ Practice your answers
- ✓ Choose an outfit appropriate for the industry to show you fit in
- ✓ Know exactly where you are going so you can arrive 5-10 minutes early

Research the company!

- Knowing about the company and its industry is impressive
- Allows you to explain how you could benefit the company
- Essential background information to look up:
  - Mission statement or values
  - Which products and services they offer
  - Company history
  - Current sales or performance
  - Who is their competition?
  - Recent news on the company

Dress for Success

Dress appropriately for the industry. Mirror the image of the people who work there, but dress <u>one step above</u> daily dress.

THEY WEAR	YOU WEAR
Uniform	Business Casual
Jeans	Business Casual
Business Casual	Business Professional
Business Professional	Business Professional

Business Casual

Ladies: Dress pants, or skirt that meets the knee, blouse (suit jacket or blazer optional) no tank tops, sandals, worn sneakers or flip flops. If wearing a skirt, wear skin colored pantyhose. Wear plain black closed-toed pumps or flats.

Gentlemen: Dress pants and a button-down shirt, polo, or sweater. Do not wear sandals or flip flops. Blazer and/or tie optional. Avoid athletic shoes. Wear plain black or brown shoes and dark socks.

Business Professional

Ladies: Dress pants or skirt that meets the knee and blouse with a suit jacket. Wear plain black closed-toed pumps.

Gentlemen: Dress pants and a button-down shirt with a tie and suit jacket. Wear plain black or brown dress shoes and dark socks.

DO	DON'T
Tuck your shirt in and wear a leather belt	Wear perfume or cologne
Wear a watch	Show piercings or tattoos
Wear natural looking makeup	Let hair hang in your face
Limit jewelry	Wear dangle or large jewelry
Looked groomed	Wear wrinkled clothes

Body Language

Non-verbal communication makes up more than half of the message we project.

Show confidence, not arrogance.

The Introduction:

Smile, shake hands, make eye contact and introduce yourself using your <u>first</u> AND <u>last name</u>

How to shake hands:

- Your hand shake should match the other person's grip, palm to palm touch and last for 3-4 shakes

Handshakes to avoid:

"the bone crusher": by squeezing too hard, this shows aggression

"dead fish": a limp hand shows lack of confidence

"dainty princess ": only offering your fingers instead of the palm show that you are apprehensive to the human touch or think you are superior

During the interview:

- Sit up straight and lean slightly forward to show interest
- Maintain good eye contact
- Avoid touching your face or folding your hands
- Don't fidget or move around in your seat

Conclusion:

- Shake hands, make eye contact and thank the interviewer for their time

Prepare for typical interview questions

Be honest, and be yourself, but a "professional version" of yourself.

Be positive and enthusiastic. Answer with examples whenever possible.

ACTIVITY: Formulate responses to each question each time you prepare for an interview. ALWAYS tailor your responses and use **relevant** experience to the position to make you the ideal person for the job.

1) **Tell me about yourself**

Do NOT answer this question with personal information!!! It needs to be about your experience.

What kind of experience have you done lately, which useful qualities or skills have you developed from these experiences? Now what, how can you apply this to this position?

_____
_____
_____
_____

Example student response:

"I am a student at_____. I am involved in team projects in my ____class where we work together to ____. I have learned the importance and benefits of team work. I know how to work together to accomplish a common goal and I look forward to applying what I learned to becoming a valuable member of this company's team."

Example job experience response:

"I have been working at _____ for ____ months. I really like working with people and have learned how to provide a great customer experience. Now I am looking for a position where I can use what I have learned in a _____environment."

<u>Tailor</u> *your response to why you want to work at the new place. Make yourself the perfect person for the job by showcasing what you have learned previously.*

2) What do you like to do in your free time?

Choose 3 things that show you are a well- rounded person. Your goal is also to try to find something you have in common with the interviewer or current team members. Pick something active or outdoors, something intellectual like reading or learning/practicing a skill, and something you like to do with friends or family.

_____
_____
_____
_____

3) What are your three greatest strengths?

Tailor these adjectives to what the position requires that you have. Use the job ad to help you!

This question may be asked in a variety of ways like give me 3 adjectives your family or friends would use to describe you. Regardless...they should be tailored to make you the perfect person for the job. Elaborate on each strength by giving an example of how you have demonstrated it through experience.

_____
_____

4) What is your greatest weakness?
Choose something you are currently struggling with and how you are working to improve. Don't choose a major requirement of the job.

_____
_____
_____

5) What is your most rewarding experience?
The employer wants to see what motivates you. Discuss something that took dedication to accomplish or made a difference to someone or your community.

_____
_____
_____
_____
_____

6) What is your ideal work environment?
Make sure your answer fits the environment of where you could be working with this company.

_____
_____
_____

7) If you were an animal which would you be and why?
Can you think on your feet? What does your answer say about your personality?

_____
_____
_____

8) Where do you see yourself 5 years from now?

Employers want to see that you have ambition. If you are a student, discuss your career plans. Try to involve this job and what you will learn in your plan. If you have a position you would like to obtain in the company, discuss this.

_____
_____
_____
_____
_____
_____

9) Have you ever had a conflict with a co-worker?

If you have, describe the experience and the steps you took to resolve the issue. If you have not, say so but explain what you WOULD do. Always take the person aside to discuss issues away from customers and co-worker. Ask for their perception without placing blame. Use a calm tone and state the issue clearly and offer possible solutions.

_____
_____
_____
_____
_____

10) Have you ever dealt with an angry customer? What did you do?

If you have, describe the experience and the steps you took to resolve the issue. If you have not, say so but explain what you WOULD do. Always show the customer that you are listening by saying "I understand" and paraphrase the issue they may be having. Talk calmly and fix the issue to the best of your ability. If you can't solve it, get a manager promptly.

_____
_____
_____
_____

11) Tell me about a time you disagreed with a decision. What did you do?
The employer wants to see that you "listen" to the other person's perspective and are able to take their opinion into consideration as well as calmly stating your own.

_____
_____
_____
_____

12) Why do you want to work here?
This is your chance to show what you know from researching the company. Show your passion for your position and describe your values that fit the company's values.

_____
_____
_____
_____
_____

13) Tell me about an achievement or goal that you have set and how you achieved it.
Give an example that can highlight your work ethic, ambition, and ability to overcome obstacles.

_____
_____
_____
_____
_____

14) Why should I hire you? OR Tell me one thing you want me to remember about you.

Summarize why you fit the team/company based on what you know about the company mission, their ad, the environment, or what they told you during the interview.

_____
_____
_____
_____
_____

Your questions for the interviewer: (MUST HAVE AT LEAST 3)

Usually at the end of the interview, they will ask if you have any questions. Prepare by writing down 4-5 in advance and bring them with you. Ask at least three that have NOT already been answered during your interview.

1) _____
2) _____
3) _____
4) What is the next step in the hiring process?   (Your last question should always be about what happens after the interview)

Suggested questions:

- What do you like most about working here?
- How do you see me fitting in with the current team?
- What are some common traits of your best employees?
- What are the day-to-day responsibilities of this job?
- What kind of opportunities exist for advancement?
- Will I be given the chance to learn new responsibilities?
- Could you describe the training period/program?
- What is the next step in the hiring process?

Conclusion of the interview: Ask for contact information such as a business card so you can follow up with a thank you note. Shake their hand, make eye contact, smile and thank them for the opportunity.

Evaluate the interview

- ✓ Do you really agree with the company mission and values?
- ✓ Do you feel like you would be a good fit for the position?
- ✓ Did you like the manager/employees?
- ✓ Do you like the environment?

> It would be better not to accept the job offer, if you don't believe you fit the organization. It would be a waste of your time and theirs. Keep looking if it's not a good fit.

Send a "thank you" after the interview

This is an opportunity to reinforce why you are qualified and interested in the position. It will demonstrate professionalism, respect and motivation. Send the thank you in an e-mail.

Example template:

Dear Mr./Ms. Last Name:

    Thank you for taking the time to discuss the _____ position with me today. I sincerely enjoyed meeting with you and learning more about the opportunity. Our conversation confirmed my interest in becoming part of _____(organization)'s staff. I was particularly excited about the opportunity to be able to_____.

    I feel confident that my experience and abilities would make me an excellent member of the organization.

    I appreciate the time you took to interview me. I look forward to hearing from you regarding your decision. If I can provide you with additional information, please let me know.

Thank you for your consideration. Sincerely,

First and Last Name

What do I do when I want to quit my job?

Tip: It is better to find another job before you quit. Never complain about your current job or manager as a reason for leaving. It should be for reasons like opportunity to learn new things or for advancement.

<u>Always</u> put it in writing!

Example letter of resignation:

Your Name
Your Phone Number
Your Email

Manager's Name
Title
Organization
Address
City, State, Zip Code

December 15, 2022 (date given to manager in person)

Dear Mr./Ms. Last Name:

I would like to inform you that I am resigning from my position as _____ at _____ (name of company), effective January 1, 2023. (2 weeks notice). Thank you for the opportunities for professional and personal development that you have provided me during the last two years. I have enjoyed working for the company and appreciate the support given to me during my employment.

If I can be of any help during this transition, please let me know.

Sincerely,

Your Signature

Your Typed Name

How do I gain experience?

How do I get experience when nobody will give me a job to get experience?

The answer: Internships and volunteer experience

Internship	Volunteer
Gain valuable skills	Gain valuable skills/experience
Usually geared toward a specific career path	Could be in any area to gain skills
Could be a paid position	Unpaid
Can lead to a paid position	Can lead to a paid position

How to get an internship:

- Internships are usually set up through your high school advisor or college career center or department chair.
- Prepare a resume tailored for an internship in a specific career field and be prepared to interview just like a traditional job
- Be sure you are working toward a degree in that field
- Do a job shadow first to make sure you are serious

How to gain volunteer experience:

- Search for an organization you feel is a worthy cause
    - www.volunteermatch.org is a great website!
- Choose something that will help you build desired skills
- Apply early to get desired hours and experience
- Be prepared to go through a training program if necessary (many have quarterly training session, so don't miss out or you may have to wait for the next one.)

<u>Every</u> experience will help you build skills toward your career path!

 **The Last Step**

Summarize it: *Write a SMART goal for your career success*

S	I will
M	To make this happen I will
A	It is attainable because
R	I will research the facts of
T	I will do this by (date)

Desired Career:_____

Desired median income: $_____

    Top 5 career values:
    1.
    2.
    3.
    4.
    5.

Possible Major(s):_____

    1st choice college:_____

    2nd choice college:_____

Bibliography

"29-1141.00." *National Center for O*NET Development.*
   https://www.onetonline.org/link/summary/29-1141.00.

"Projections of occupational employment, 2016–26," Career Outlook, U.S. Bureau of Labor Statistics, October
   2017. https://www.bls.gov/careeroutlook/2017/article/occupational-projections-charts.htm.

"Higher Education Admission Requirements." (2015). Colorado Department of Higher Education.
   March 30. http://highered.colorado.gov/academics/admissions/coursecompletion.html.

"How Aid is Calculated." *Federal Student Aid: Office of the U.S. Department of Education.*
   https://studentaid.ed.gov/sa/fafsa/next-steps/how-calculated

"My Next Move." *National Center for O*NET Development.* http://www.mynextmove.org/.

Metcalf, T. "Listening to Your Clients, Life Association News 92, no. 7 (1997): 16-18

Mohs, Richard C. "How Human Memory Works" (2007). *HowStuffWorks.com.*
   http://science.howstuffworks.com/life/inside-the-mind/human-brain/human-memory.htm

"My MBTI Results." *The Myers & Briggs Foundation.* (2014).
   http://www.myersbriggs.org/my-mbti-personality-type/my-mbti-results/

"O*NET Interest Profiler." *National Center for O*NET Development.*
   http://www.mynextmove.org/explore/ip>

"Secondary School Teachers." *National Center for O*NET Development.*
   http://www.mynextmove.org/profile/summary/25-2031.00>.

"Types of Aid." *Federal Student* Aid: Office of the U.S. Department of Education.
   https://studentaid.ed.gov/sa/types.

WHEN I TELL PEOPLE ABOUT WHAT I TEACH THEY ALWAYS SAY:

"I WISH I HAD A CLASS LIKE THAT IN HIGH SCHOOL"

WELL…NOW YOU CAN HAVE IT TOO!

ABOUT THE AUTHOR

I have been coaching High School students on college and career success for almost 20 years. I became inspired by my own mistakes in my career path. I originally went to college to pursue a career in broadcasting when I realized it wasn't for me. In hindsight, I realized I was in it for the wrong reasons. My goal is to give students the tools they need to make the right decisions to reach their own personal, educational and career goals. My mother always told me I should write a book, I guess I finally listened to her!

Made in the USA
Las Vegas, NV
05 August 2022